¡DIVAS!

Nuala Ní Chonchúir

Editor

¡DIVAS!

A Sense of Place

ARLEN
HOUSE

ISBN 1–903631–45–9, paperback

First published by Arlen House in April 2005

Arlen House
PO Box 222
Galway
Ireland

Phone/fax: 086 8207617
Email: arlenhouse@ireland.com

Typesetting: Arlen House
Front cover painting by Maura Flannery
Back cover painting by Stef Callaghan
Printed by: Betaprint, Dublin

contents

¡DIVAS!: A Sense of Place is a bilingual portrait of contemporary women's writing in Galway, featuring poetry, fiction, drama, memoir, song-writing and translation. This volume was commissioned by Arlen House to celebrate the 30th birthday of the press' foundation in Galway in 1975. We invited 50 of our favourite writers to submit material for this anthology - the second in the critically-acclaimed *¡DIVAS!* series. Alongside the more established names, this cross-generational anthology showcases some of the county's emerging and less well-known voices; the calibre of their work augers well for the future of women's writing in Galway and in Ireland.

It is acknowledged that writers notice more than other people - that they are compelled to set down their 'noticings' and their feelings about the world, using apt imagery and arresting language. A love of words - of language itself - surely has to be one of the central motivators at the heart of every writer. The contributors to this anthology display a passion for noticing the small details of life and for telling their stories - in poetry, drama and prose - through beautiful language. Dolores Stewart's combined use of intellect and evocative word-choice, to relay the story of a Dutch woman killed in Auschwitz, is a pure illustration of this:

Fiú amháin in Auschwitz
Na h-aimhleasa, ag deireadh lae,

Anseo láithreach insna críocha déanacha
I gcroílár dhubhfhocail an chéasta,

Bímse ag spágáil amach romham
Faoi chamscáth na sreinge deilgní,

Scéal earraigh i mo chéim is port úrnua
Leathchumtha i ndúrún mo chroí.

Diversity of style and content are the essence and nature of any anthology, even one with a unified theme. Place - in the theme 'a sense of place' - was widely interpreted by the contributors. Some, like Breid Sibley, opt for the physical place, the home:

The stones and earth in my garden
hold their memories
cowslips, daisies, corn flowers
forget-me-nots blossom
before the grass is cut
my bones remember ...

Others yearn for a place left behind, as in Jessie Lendennie's *Exile Sequence*:

Landscape?
Oh, yes, I miss the landscape
who would forget Great Salt Lake
or the Greyhound bus station at El Paso.
So many images, yes, and they haunt me
haunting as any puzzle or paradox.

A thread of honesty and authenticity runs through all of the work here: the writers dive in and explore what it means to be a woman in twenty-first century Ireland. There is an abundance of self-analysis, of finding one's own place in love, in lust, in family life; we find stories of mothers and fathers, abusers and the abused, immigrants and blow-ins, lovers and spouses, lonely children and lonelier adults.

Thankfully, there is a healthy wryness evident in much of the work, particularly in the writings of Pat Jourdan, Maureen Gallagher and Marion Moynihan, all of whom relish the use of humour, coupled with delicate language, to make their points. Consider an extract from Maureen Gallagher's *Once I was a Child*:

> I discovered failure when I was seven and they asked me to sing *Adeste Fidelis*. It was Christmas and money was short and families had to make their own entertainment. De Valera had great time for church and family ... Anyway, I sang like a nightingale, and they laughed until they cried.
>
> Children were a great source of entertainment in those days. I gave up singing afterwards. I gave up believing in fairies and bogeymen around the same time, but this being Ireland, God took longer.

Writing in the *New York Times*, Margo Jefferson likened poets to aerialists, stating that 'the wire they walk stretches from history to eternity, fact to dream, language to silence. When they get across we feel rapture. They've taken us with them'. It is easy to substitute 'writers' for 'poets' in relation to the work in this volume: time and again the reader will be transported from the past to the present on a high-wire of vibrant images, deep emotion, intricate language and memorable stories.

We are honoured to include in this volume the work of the late Bríd Cummins, side by side with Rita Ann Higgins' powerful poem *Return To Sender*. It is also our pleasure to feature work by Anne Kennedy, including the wonderful, previously unpublished, poem *On Seeing Máirtín Ó Direáin Strolling in Salthill*.

Bain sult as!
Enjoy!
Mo bhuíochas

Nuala Ní Chonchúir

Loughrea, Co Galway
March 2005

acknowledgements

Jessie Lendennie, Publisher of Salmon Poetry and Deirdre Ní Thuathail, Publisher of Clo Iar-Chonnachta, who have published books by many of the authors featured in this anthology.

Irish language specialists, Róisín Ní Mhianáin and Micheál Ó Conghaíle; Pádraig Ó hAoláin, Údarás na Gaeltachta and Majella Ní Chríocháin, Ealaín na Gaeltachta, for helping us to locate and publish Irish language writers.

Maura Kennedy and staff at the Galway Arts Centre, and the Cúirt advisory committee.

Angela Harte and family
Rita Ann Higgins

Nollaig Mac Congáil
John Dillon
Andrew Brock
Matthew at Dubray Books
Eileen Foley
Tom Kenny
Stef Callaghan
Maura Flannery

All the authors who contributed so swiftly and so warmly to our invitation to submit work for consideration.

Anne Kennedy

(1935-1998)

ON SEEING MÁIRTÍN Ó DIREÁIN STROLLING IN SALTHILL

for Jack Mitchell

I

In my youth I saw Máirtín Ó Direáin
strolling in Salthill in a long black
coat and broad-brimmed hat
like Gulliver or a priest gone daft.

He ambled so smoothly he could have been
on tracks, his poet's hands clasped
loosely behind his back, his gaze
fixed past the middle distance.

Perhaps it was the horizon he saw that day
where the islands lolled in sun and mist
against a white sheet only a realist
would take for a sky.

And who was I? A young housewife who'd
never read a line of his, much less
attempted verse myself, and yet I sensed
I was seeing greatness.

He was walking towards the sea,
I was walking home.
Next time he passes, I promised,
I'll snap his portrait from the back,

The broad coat and hat a shadow,
drama itself. And if I'm lucky
I'll get his autograph. Though I looked
and looked, I never saw him pass.

For years I wondered why a man with Aran
in his blood bothered with the mainland
at all. Vague notions of the civil
service or the bank sufficed.

II

One wet Sunday I unearth
on brittle newsprint, an interview
Ó Direáin gave before he died.
Slow and steady yet again.

He wonders if they still speak poetry
on Aran; admires Synge
because he cared; hears Yeats
early and late, even in his dreams.

His one wish was to be like Pearse
but his mother all but cosseted
the manhood out of him.
He was meant to be a priest

Or guard, not some loner
watching under lowering skies
loaded currachs bumping
stone quays on Aran.

Growing up to exile with stones
and mountainous seas for companions,
where else would he dwell
except in Death's lonely kingdom.

(May 1997)

1.

The road to Buck Mountain
ends at my cabin.
From the cliff it appears
to travel underwater and surface
as the lights that fly up the ski run
above Vancouver.
Last night my road sliced the sky
all the way to the Arctic;
my neighbour called it the Northern Lights.

...

5.

In search of trout
I walk up a steep logging trail.
The spring air spins out a frail heat.
Halfway up Buck Mountain I discover a pond
and catch dinner.
When my neighbour later boasts
he owns my hidden pond,
'man-made and routinely stocked',
imagine my dismay.

BURIAL INSTRUCTIONS

I don't want to be cremated,
my clothes sent home in a bag,
my ashes sifted from the furnace grate
for my Claddagh ring
and gold fillings.

No, plant me,
like my Grandmother's blazing dahlias
in the subsuming earth,
where I can be lifted,
where there's a chance of resurrection.

How about the hump-backed hill
beyond Barna
riddled with Celtic crosses,
or the sun-shot meadow on Orcas
facing steaming Mt. Baker.

On second thought
Westwood is best,
beside my mother
where the mocking-bird sang
the night she was buried.
You might know the spot
because that's where they placed
Marilyn's ashes
in a pale marble crypt
looking across at our family plot.

They say it's Joe
provides the perpetual rose,
but no one knows for certain.
Be sure you put me in the ground
where I will have a chance to rise.

THE DOG KUBLA DREAMS MY LIFE

I acquired you, old companion,
on impulse from the Palo Alto pound
to satisfy an adolescent
urge for someone all my own.

You crouched shivering on the back
seat of my black '48 Chevy, shedding
fair hair, your obsidian toe-
nails slipping on slick upholstery.

Transported into the redwoods
you tore off down the old highway,
a gold whipcord,
lured back with a bit of steak.

In the cabin bathroom, your corner
stake-out made ferny wastes our outdoor
toilet, as you snarled comic guarding
your own ceramic reservoir.

Tamed with coos and coaxings
into a loyalty hard-won,
I called you *Kubla*
after that nervy invader.

In an attic in Berkeley, you shredded
the socks of my first lover, pawed
ravelled strands beside my rumpled bed,
then patrolled the narrow stairs.

Pacing the pine floor-boards, those wolfish
toes tip-tapped a sentry song. Nobody's guide
dog, you wore no harness, roamed at will.
You could be gone for days prowling

lanes and harbour wastelands or snoozing
contented in some student's kitchen.
They called *Kubla* on Telegraph Avenue,
you glinted sidelong.

When I moved to L.A. I entrusted you to a friend
until I settled in where dogs were welcome.
He said you got lost, wandered off, followed
some family back up to the redwoods.

He claimed I had made you too friendly.
Year later I heard you were killed
the week I left,
running towards a woman
calling *Kubla* from the kerb.

Anne Kennedy (née Hoag) was born in Los Angeles in 1935. She was educated at Stanford and worked as a high school teacher and freelance journalist. With her close friend, Rex Stewart, a former trumpet player in the Duke Ellington Band, she recorded a series of interviews with jazz musicians which is now housed in Ellington's archive in the Smithsonian Museum of American History. She moved to the San Juan Islands in the Pacific Northwest in 1972 and from there to Galway in 1977. A talented photographer, her work includes a series inspired by Nora Barnacle and another by Irish proverbs. Her first poetry collection, *Buck Mountain Poems* (Salmon, 1989) was inspired by the thousand year old *Cold Mountain Poems* by the Chinese poet Han Shan and is set in the San Juan Islands. Her second volume, *The Dog Kubla Dreams My Life* (Salmon, 1994), is a haunting exploration of memory and belonging, notable for its fragile and evocative imagery. Anne Kennedy died in 1998 and is survived by four daughters and a son.

Eva Bourke

POEMS FOUND ON A STRAND IN MANNIN BAY

for Leo Hallissey

I

Cells

On the coral strand near Shannanagower
I found a piece of what I thought
was washed-up Styrofoam -
it lay on my palm
white and weighing nothing at all
as though made of rice
paper, the merest breeze
could have blown it away -
roughly the size of a tennis-ball,
a little misshapen and subdivided
into multiple cells,
and I was told it was the egg case
of the common whelk.

But what is common about a creature
that hatches from such airy
and otherworldly honeycombs
and floats to the ocean ground
to grow itself a house with winding stair
and a whorl around the door,
the inside walls mother-of-pearl?

II

Purses

All the children searched the drift-line
for mermaid's purses that afternoon,
inky, foursquare, antlered and tough
like a witch's uterus,
or oblong pouches with spiral-haired floats
made of taffeta, as though
dropped and forgotten by water sprites.

They clambered over rocks and beach
calling exultantly like the sedge-
warbler across the fields. The catch
of skate and dogfish flitting through the depths
was far beyond their reach.

III

Casings

A crab's casing, recently abandoned
floats in the littoral surf.
Cannier than any other thing
on this strand, the crab
has just lifted the curve
of the lid and climbed
out of its own shell
and laterally sidled off.
I turn the armour, dark green buff
and dank as moss
with its limp appendices
of legs and shears, to gaze
at the gothic grimace
of its face. The dead eyes
on their stalks stare at me
as though crazed.

IV
Shells

We crossed over to Omey Island Indian file
through two fingers of water, half a mile
on the vast stretch of sand
between Omey and mainland.
Dogs and children racing ahead plus
the larks spinning out their cavatinas
provided an ambient island music
of twitter, dog bark, high melodic

cries, grass scent and pollen lay thick
in the air, a stonewall formed the backdrop
to some in-depth expert look
at flora, lichen, rock.
Within minutes we were prostrate
like Muslim penitents on our knees
to worship through magnifying glasses
the Persian miniature plants and grasses.

the densely woven prayer carpet
studded with the chalk-white shells
of the incumbent Omey snail:
lady's bedstraw, all bristling stalks
at give or take an inch and a half,
the machair fern, a lilliputian phallus,
between the cranebill's microscopic flowers
the scarlet pinheads of the pimpernel.

The larks played curtain-raisers all the while
to some bigwig herring gull's
dramatics in the aquatinted sky -
old hands at the annual summer show biz -
letting their high-flown tautologies
tell you this world is all there is.

THE LAST HOUSE

after Rainer Maria Rilke

No matter who you are, when evening comes
get up and leave your room with the familiar
things, scattered books, photographs
pinned to the shelves,
no matter who you are.

And as you step outside into a lively scene
of buildings, people, traffic rushing past,
it strikes you that your house is last
before the empty distances begin,

and though you're tired beyond words,
your eyes too tired to lift themselves across
the busy threshold of your house,
yet they'll slowly raise aloft a tree
and place it standing straight against the sky,
black, slim and solitary,

and you have made the world anew,
and it is vast and silent,
a word picked early as a fruit
that's left to ripen in the sun.

But at the moment when
you think you've understood
what it all means, your eyes
let go of it again with tenderness.

HYPERION'S SONG OF DESTINY

Translation of Friedrich Hölderlin

You dwell in the light.
  You walk on soft ground, blessed spirits!
    Bright heavenly breezes
      Touch you lightly
        Like the musician's fingers
          Her sacred strings.

Without past or future, the gods
  Draw breath like the slumbering infant.
    Their souls flower
      Eternally forth
        From the pristine
          And cherished bud.
            And their blissful gaze
              Is filled with a tranquil
                Timeless light.

But for us is ordained
  To have nowhere to rest.
    Human and frail,
      We vanish and topple
        Blindly from hour
          To hour like water
            Flung from rockface
              To rockface, year
                After year, into the uncertain void.

Aunt Svea

Translation of Lars Gustafsson

She lived for eighty-six years.
Strictly speaking not for very long.
(If you look at it within a larger context.)
In the winter of 1919 she was a small Smålandic girl
who was delighted with her new shoes.
(She had never got new shoes before)
until she dried her shoes
over the red-hot oven in school
and found that the soles
were made of card board.

In her stockings she walked
home through the whirling snow drifts.
So I was told.

And, hardworking and bitter,
she lived for another 80 years
in the end sitting lonely and childless
in her dark kitchen.

Eva Bourke is originally from Germany and has lived in Galway for many years. She is married to Eoin Bourke and they have three children. Eva is the author of *Gonella* (Salmon, 1985), *Litany for the Pig* (Salmon, 1989), *Spring in Henry Street* (Dedalus, 1996), *Travels with Gandolpho* (Dedalus, 2000) and has translated the poet Elisabeth Borchers in *Winter on White Paper* (Dedalus, 2002). She has also compiled two anthologies of contemporary Irish poetry translated into German. Her latest collection, *The Latitude of Naples* (Dedalus), is launched in April 2005 at the Cúirt Festival in Galway.

Mary O'Malley

AT THE FORGE
An extract from a memoir of place

Winter or summer, the door of the forge never closed and
the fire inside was never quenched for long. This was
where dirty bits of iron were changed and turned into
lovely shiny objects, where she first learned the meaning of
the word 'wrought'. She didn't know then, nor for a long
time to come, that the word for the man who made boats,
boat-wright, came from the same stem. To get to the forge
she left her house, walked past the cowshed, past the big
field full of nettles, past the thatched house on the left with
its out-houses and stalls for cattle and the horse, and on to
the end of the boreen. She turned left, breasted the big hill,
then walked down the slope and over to Lydon's corner.
Dun Hill rose like a whale in front and on a clear day the
castle on its gentler slope was mirrored in the lake.

The first time she went she had to be accompanied by
one of the men or an older cousin. Later, when she started
school she would often go alone. Sometimes she asked to
go to the Seven Sisters' Well first. If she was let, she
climbed over the wall at Lydon's, and into the world of
trees. There were no trees anywhere else in the village and
she knew rich people must have lived there. In a clearing,
the ruins of the house stood behind a sort of lawn. Rusted
stumps in concrete marked the place where the gate used
to be and the house no longer had a roof. In June she went
there for the scent of roses, which drifted out towards her,
slightly purple and velvety like the flowers themselves.

She entered the house, sometimes stepping through
the walls like a small trespassing ghost, sometimes
entering through the front door as if she owned the
place. She walked from bedroom to kitchen to a room

that must have been the parlour, and out again. Hurrying now, she skirted the side of the house and walked along a rough path, over a stone wall and into the field to the blessed well. She knelt and said her prayers, racing through them, then blessed herself with speed. The wet greenness over the water was strewn with buttons and statues and bits of broken rosary beads, with the faint peeling lustre of pearls which shone from within like small misshapen moons. Once a brooch was left as an offering in one of the mossy clefts, in another a tiny statue of St. Anthony and a chalky headless statue of the infant of Prague, the blush still pink on his flaking cheeks. On each visit, she left an offering: ribbons, a hairgrip, a green slide and once, a whole sixpence for a very special intention.

Coins and miraculous medals glinted at the bottom of the well. It was always quiet and peaceful there. Sometimes children went there together on the way home from school and nobody shouted or raised their voices until they left the circle of the well. She thought they were like the children in the leaflets about Our Lady of Fatima and they talked about what would happen if Our Lady appeared to them and would they be frightened if the sun started circling in the sky. It never did though, and no-one appeared to them, not even a saint.

In May, a froth of whitethorn covered the bushes. This was closely followed by the thick creamy hawthorn, which turned this desolate place into somewhere else, into a garden in a storybook. The blossom surged out of winter in such profusion she imagined it covering the walls, the ruined house, the road itself. What if it forgot to stop? What if it kept coming and smothered the world? It made the air taste rich and heady. She always knew it wouldn't last and it never did. Each month the bushes and flowers were different. You couldn't bring whitethorn inside the door but she watched, every June, for the coming of the roses. She picked them, pricking her fingers on the thorns, then brought them home and placed them in a jam-jar of water on the windowsill. When the roses were gone she picked big daisies and sprays of Mont Bretia, which flamed on the sage-green mantelpiece. When all else failed there were cowslips, and sprigs of fuschia. The little girls picked off the pink outer leaves and attached them to their fingertips with spit and simpered. The pointed leaves were waxy and rich and fell off as soon as they dried. When the girls tired of this, they tried to make the flowers dangle from their ears. This was less successful, but it was the beginning of glamour.

Now it was September and she was on her own. She made her visit and ate handfuls of glistening blackberries. When she emerged onto the road again, her mouth and hands were dyed purple. Hurrying, she heard the bright clang of metal being struck on the anvil before she reached the forge, and the blue light of the welding rod flashed out like a lightning tree, shorting and sparking. This was not the same as the light of the sun. It was hard and dangerous as if real lightning had been captured and trapped in those thin grey rods. When it got out you could hear its wild sizzle.

She looked into the darkened forge, carefully as she had been taught, to avoid the direct glare. The smith was a short man. He wore a special apron to protect his clothes. It was black and shiny down the front, from the anvil and from the horses hooves rubbing against the leather when he held them against him as he pulled out the old nails, and took off their worn out shoes.

This was the best place. This was where ugly lumps of metal were changed by fire and made into tulips for candlesticks, beautiful gates and the many kinds of horseshoes that were displayed above the big door which rolled along on a track, opening almost the whole front of the forge to the daylight. Inside there were shadows and mysteries. She knew nothing about what was called the elemental then, only the tingle along her skin at the chaos and the fire and the bright loud sounds of metal striking metal. So she watched the shapes emerging, her uncle holding a great square mask before his eyes. She had to look away while he was welding, though once he had let her hold the mask, just to see what it was like, how to darken a world too bright to look on for long.

Her back to the work, she saw the magnesium light flash around the walls, heard the waspy sound then turned to see the joining scar raised on the metal like a poker burn on skin. This was filed neatly, with a grating sound and sure strokes.

When she was lucky, the horses came. They allowed the smith to go right in behind their huge front legs. She stood well back, while her uncle lifted each hoof in turn and worked at it like a dentist at a tooth. He pared them and tapped the shoes that had been especially made for them into place with special flat nails. She was afraid that the horse would be hurt, a nail driven too far in. The horse's eyes pleaded, like Christ in 'The Agony in the Garden'. They were big liquid eyes. Sometimes the horse whinnied and stamped at first, but her uncle wasn't afraid and soon the animal stood quietly while the owner talked softly about fishing and the shower in the government and the nails were hammered in without any pain at all. Final adjustments were made and the fit declared comfortable. The horse would whinny, toss back his head and clomp away, the new set of silver shoes sparking on the road, twisting and showing off like a big girl.

Then she examined the anvil, and a high workbench fitted with metal grips. Sometimes she was let turn the big screw and place a piece of timber under it. Jim showed her how to tighten it just the right amount but she wasn't very good. She preferred to play with the big pile of iron filings, heavy as blackened sand, teasing them, making them move as slowly as she could until all of a sudden they rushed to the big horseshoe-shaped magnet, and clung, unable to resist. Magnetism. Jim explained it to her. She imagined a big field, perfectly oblong, with the magnets sticking up like lumps of rock, somewhere near the North Pole. It was called the magnetic field and it was so powerful, it gave force to all the magnets in the world, in forges and batteries and cars, even the little play ones they got as toys. The rock magnets were brown but the rest of the field was covered in moss. She knew it was ice, more likely, but it was hard to imagine a field of ice. She tried. The picture in her mind was too cold and it was a bad colour. Moss was better, with all the little filings rushing across the white expanse of the far north, like tiny rabbits, desperate to get home to their green velvety mother lode.

She'd wait around the forge forever in the hopes Jim would say 'Do you want to work the bellows?' The hearth was a few feet above floor level with an aperture for the air to come through. The bellows blew into that. She'd look to her uncle for approval, then stretching as high up as she could, onto her toes even, she grasped the wooden handle and pulled down with her full weight, straining her arms and her chest. She'd hang there for one silent moment of struggle, then the great lung began to empty and sparks came from the bottom of the fire as she bore down. The handle would lift up and swing her with it. The struggle was repeated and the fire puffed again. Now she had rhythm. She set the fire blazing and her uncle added coal and later slack. When he said 'Good girl, that's enough', she stopped and wriggled her toes in her brown robin sandals, pleased, liking this more than any of the knitting or sewing she knew she'd never be able to master and never did.

Mary O'Malley is the author of four collections of poetry published by Salmon Press and *The Boning Hall: New and Selected Poems* published by Carcanet. She grew up in Connemara, has received a Hennessy award for her poetry, as well as three Arts Council bursaries.

She travels regularly to the United States and Europe to read her work and lecture on contemporary Irish poetry. She lived in Lisbon for eight years and has edited three anthologies of new writing, including *The Waterside Book* which arose out of a residency in the Verbal Arts Centre. She broadcasts regularly on radio and recently presented a series of six programmes drawing on her interest in working with musicians and young people.

She was closely involved with the organisation of the Cúirt Literature Festival for many years, programming both the regular festival and initiating and developing its educational programme. She regularly participates in both Letterfrack Sea Week and Bog Week and the Clifden Community Arts week.

Her collection, *The Knife in the Wave*, deals with what she sees as the threat to a city and its way of life from economic greed and questions Galway's image of itself as a city of the arts, while *Asylum Road* addresses the changing Ireland and in particular the new Irish. She has been Mayo Writer-in-Residence and held residencies in the Verbal Arts Centre in Derry, in Manhattanville University in New York, in Ty Newwydd in Wales and unofficially in the Aran Islands, where she has aided the writer's group for many years. She has recenly formed links with Spanish, French, Corsican and Portuguese poets through PEN Clube International. Some of her poems have been translated into French, Portuguese, Italian, among other languages. She has worked on translations from a number of languages, most recently the poems of Pura Lopes Colome.

She has two children, lives in Galway and is a member of Aosdana. She was 2003 writer in residence in the Irish Cultural Centre in Paris and has been Director of the Douglas Hyde Conference for the past two years.

Celia de Fréine

morning ireland

An dara lá den bhriseadh
lár téarma agus mé traochta.

Ach níl orm éirí. Níl orm
éinne a dhíláithriú as a leaba.

Is féidir luí siar i gcomhluadar
an nuachtóra is scinneadh

thar muir is thar tír ar thóir
an scannail is deireanaí.

Néal ag titim arm nuair a sciurdann
na focail Frith-D tharam.

Cuirtear agallamh ar dhochtúir
ach ní thuigim a bhfuil á rá aici:

instelladh glóbailin thruaillithe
sna mílte ban

ar bhuail an galar buí grupaí díobh.

scéal scéil

Dar leis na tuairiscí raidió
tá na hospidéil tar éis litreacha
a chur chuig na mná uilig

ar tugadh an ghlóbailin amhrasach dóibh.
Ó tharla gur bhog muidne
caithfidh go ndeachaigh mo litirse ar strae.

Cuirim scairt ar an ospidéal.
Fiafraíonn siad díom ar chuala mé
faoin scéal ar an nuacht.

Ar an nuacht a chuala siadsan faoi freisin.
B'in an chéad uair a chuala siad faoi.
Má thagaim isteach amárach

déanfaidh siad tástáil fola orm.
Má thagaim isteach amárach
seans go mbeidh leid acu céard atá ag tarlú.

At the time I thought it strange
that he should sit beside me
when the rest of the upper deck
was empty but I kept on peering
out the window, sniffing the goose-
eggs from the Monument Creamery,
the cream doughnuts and coffee
from Ferguson's. As the bus came
even with Lees' and I glimpsed
the plimsolls that would be mine
on Friday, I felt the nudge of his elbow.

Too shy to face him I glanced down
and saw that other eye glisten.
I heard the leather of the conductor's
shoes on the metal of the stairs,
the clink of coins in the leather
of his bag and in the long pause
before he said *fares please*
I waited to be rescued, to watch
as he wrestled this fellow passenger
to the floor. A tanner was proffered,
the dial on the dispenser clicked
into place, a ticket severed. The steps
of the navy blue official retreated
and with them my trust in uniform
was sucked into the vortex of the stairwell.

The bus continued on past the gents' toilet,
the Garda Station, and as the Church
of the Three Patrons came into view,
I rose and said *excuse me please*
as I had been taught. I can still see,
as he stood aside, not so much that glisten,

or the maroon fuzz-framed erectness
that sprang from between his flies,
but the blue of his gaze - a clear cobalt
that stared straight ahead.

HIGH STREET

You watch your dream-flakes flurried up
into a whirlpool of beings
that will descend again tonight

and submerge you in eau-de-Nil
where children splash and there's no sand
to walk on. Because she preferred

the city you'll lead her through streets
where shops huddle, their arched doorways
drawing you both into the warmth

and bustle of bargains. A clutch
bag in turquoise with a garnet
stud like one in her mother's ring

will be fingered and then replaced.
She'll disclose she already owns
its mate though you know she's not been

abroad in ages. Together
you'll unfurl a child's kingfisher
cloak into a memory sea

where tears crystallize in borders
and happy days poise on clasps
that glint in the light's fluorescence.

BULGARIAN RHAPSODY

For Dora and Lyubomir

1

High on Sophia street lamps
storks build their nest,
unaware a new era has come.

Chicks hatch above twenty-fourth
of May High School balloons
and jubilation. Why all the fuss?

Mother swathes her young
for the journey between
one high-rise block and another.

She taps on windows,
wondering why so few
are prepared to accept her gift.

2

Bishop John has prepared figs
grown on sacred ground,
sweetened with Rozhen honey.

We sip water from blue glasses
on a gallery forbidden to tourists.
Beneath us an apricot tree

and potted irises feed on drizzle.
The air is so fresh I can scarcely
breathe. In the courtyard

a butterfly perches on my wrist -
I recognise her familiar
form: *Mother, your taste,*

as ever, is impeccable, your timing
perfect. I haven't forgotten
those journeys you never made,

the clothes you bought
but never wore. These navy socks
are yours, as is the olive fleece.

In the Church of Mary's Birth
I rest my palm on the silver
of the icon's hand and wish.

3

Above the Rhodope Mountains
young clouds flee their mothers'
care, to sport and tittle-tattle

over derelict schools,
deserted villages. Some,
when caught and scolded,

shed tears on shoots that rent
the cobblestones. Others stray
far from home, like legions lost

to America, their loneliness
engulfed by the Chepelarska
as it gorges down to the plain.

4

When I return home sleep
comes to me - a lover,
strong and dark, who chinks

through shutters and lies
by my side. His lips nuzzle
the down on my neck

bolting all that had drained
my strength. Together
we lie late, when children

are at school, and dogs
snooze. We stretch our limbs
and pin posters to the sky.

Celia de Fréine is a poet and dramatist. She was born in Northern Ireland and now lives in Dublin and in Connemara. Two collections of poetry in Irish, *Faoi Chabáistí is Ríonacha* (2001) and *Fiacha Fola* (2004) have been published by Cló Iar-Chonnachta. A collection in English *Scarecrows at Newtownards* is due in 2005. Her poetry has won several awards, including the Patrick Kavanagh Award and Gradam Litríochta Chló Iar-Chonnachta. Her play *Anraith Neantóige* was produced by *Aisling Ghéar* in 2004. She has twice won the Oireachtas na Gaeilge award for best play. She was awarded Arts Council Bursaries in 1997 and in 2000.

Pat Jourdan

TRANSUBSTANTIATION-MEANS-INSTEAD

Easy, easy, to gobble down the words
along with the fairy-stories,
school rules and poetry.
Horses stomping woody floors -
or not writing in the margin -
or the robber-girl and rubies.
So Jesus turning himself into bread
was just as normal as all the rest.
Even through the sieve of exams
the idea remained. I had faith
untested, unaware, an incidental pagan.
Only this instant, kneeling at the bench,
I catch sight of the hosts carried to the altar,
before their change
(flat, creamy paper coins
sticking to each other)
safe in their golden universe
always gold on the inside,
even the pre-god demands this.
Dust-motes sparkle in the beam
Of April sunlight; so near, so almost rude,
Like seeing dandruff close up.

An ordinary woman holds the ciborium,
an ordinary man beside her has the wine.
They speed on, up to the altar.

Soon all hell will let loose.
Centuries through, our differences.

My mother used to go berserk
when I coughed up blood.
I didn't care. To a child
the coloured gobs looked pretty,
yellow, orange, vermilion,
they contained pools. Mine.
parts of me exploding out
into the white enamel bowl.
Wet patches, first paintings
never bettered.

A PREGNANT WOMAN SURVEYS THE RUSH-HOUR

Which is the greater miracle,
the plum-ripe belly,
or that these grey figures
twice daily
disappear down tunnels through the city,
mute moles?

A field, a green field,
a field with a horse in it,
a white horse against the driving rain
with a wind-shorn tree in the sunset.
Some mountains;
settled in blue distance, a white cottage.
More fields scattered as far as the eye can see.
Weather (rain, hail, sun, mist)
and time (seasons, stars, moon, etc.)
provided free, self-maintaining.
The reader the only occupant
except perhaps some suitable peasants
going about their picturesque peasant-humble tasks,
off-centre, middle distance, blurred,
and of course, the patient horse,
the myriad, puzzling green vanishing points.

Pat Jourdan, poet and fiction writer, was born in Liverpool where she qualified as a painter. She lived in Galway until recently; she has now returned to England. She has won the Molly Keane Award for fiction and the Cootehill Poetry Award. Her latest poetry collection is *Turpentine* (Motet Press, 2004), and her work appears in *Anthology 1* from Ainnir.

Gabrielle Warnock

THE HOMECOMING

I have difficulty in recognising my daughter Kathy as I stand on tip-toes, craning my neck to get a view of the passengers from her flight milling into the enclosed baggage area of the arrivals lounge. At first I think that she must have missed her flight, and I realise that I am not just thinking it. I am hoping it. The realization shows me how I have been dreading her return. When I finally do recognise her, I realise that her return is going to be far worse than I had anticipated.

While away, she has shaved off most of her hair. One section has been left to form a thin plait which dangles forwards over her left eye and is secured by an elasticated ring of what look like red beads, though it is difficult to be sure from this distance. I find myself wondering how on earth I am going to bring her to lunch with her grandmother (whose opinions have grown sharper and less tolerant with the passing years and whose appreciation of Kathy has long since dissipated).

Kathy's face, in the height of summer, so far as I can see, is painted a luminous white (though the luminosity may be exaggerated by the very bright lights which shine overhead). She is standing with her arm linked into that of a man who wears a beard and small, very pointed shoes. She is taller than he is. I am annoyed because I am not expecting a man. She has not told me that there is another man. I wave at her through the locked glass doors as she waits to collect her suitcases from the crawling belt of luggage and she twiddles her fingers back at me, then turns away. She speaks to her friend and points towards me. He looks at me and I smile as befits the mother of his girl-friend, but he has looked away again before he notices and the smile is wasted.

I don't feel like smiling. I am tired of the succession of men. I am wearied of attempting to like them all, of trying to convince myself of their good points, of trying to imagine them as husbands to my daughter (because, though she denies it, she is looking for a man to marry), only to find them departed and replaced. Doubtless I did the same myself, but I can't remember being so unbalanced by them. And did I have so many? Of course, I didn't go to bed with them all. She has no restraint and what I resent more than anything else is her compulsion to talk to me. Perhaps I am an unnatural mother, but I don't want her confidences. I have no desire to hear sexual details and I have no advice to offer.

The young man's name is Winchy. His real name is William but this he has eschewed in favour of something more winsome. He says he finds William too redolent of Scott Fitzgerald and long scarves. We are carrying luggage out to the car park while he talks and I nod and say that I see what he means, since I have only just met him and hardly wish to begin with an argument. Besides, I seem to have picked up the heaviest suitcase and I am too puffed to speak. I can't precisely recall Scott Fitzgerald's novels, but the name William does not ring a bell and I make a mental note that I must check him out.

Winchy seems to be much the same as all the others. Apart from the American intonations there is nothing specific to single him out. He plays the piano, but most of them played something. Frank used to play the violin (quite well) and even Poddy played the recorder (appallingly). Kathy says that they sometimes try duets, though he is far more advanced than she is. We have a piano at home on which Kathy struggled half-heartedly as a child. I remember I was encouraging for a time, but then I lost heart myself because she was so reluctant to learn. It takes love, it seems.

'I've never been to Ireland before', Winchy says as we drive back towards Dublin.

He is sitting in the back of the car, but it hardly seems like it as he has both arms draped over Kathy's shoulders and one hand is playing with the red beads around her plait, while the other holds her hand. His head is pressed against hers, obliterating my vision through the rear-view mirror. I feel very crowded. 'I don't even have an Irish relative. My ancestors are mostly Italian, I believe'.

Which explains the lack of height. And even the pointed shoes? But I mustn't be catty. He has spent a great deal of money to come over here for a holiday with my daughter. At least, I suppose he has come for no more than a holiday. I take a quick look sideways and see to my relief that Kathy wears no rings on her fingers. Not that rings would mean anything either way, but it is something.

She has been in the States six months and in that six months has only written to me on two occasions, though she did ring me once, for my birthday, which touched me, even though she had mis-calculated the time difference and I was woken at three o'clock in the morning.

I wish she had warned me about her hair. I find her appearance such a shock. I can't understand why she should deliberately have marred her looks. I haven't mentioned it to her, because I can't think what I can possibly say that won't sound either critical or hypocritical. When I hugged her in the arrivals hall my face was prickled by the stubble of hair which is bristling like the beginnings of a beard all over her head. I noticed that she scratches her scalp quite a lot, and I remember, from childbirth, that freshly growing hair tickles. Perhaps she is going to allow it to grow back to normal. Then I begin to worry that the hair will have changed colour. She has, or had, the most beautiful hair. A burnished patina of gold fused with red.

It is still only breakfast time when we arrive home. I have laid in rashers especially, but neither of them want more than toast and coffee. Winchy says they ate trash throughout the flight, because they couldn't sleep. They were in the front seats, right under the film screen, so that they couldn't see the picture, but they were kept awake by the sound. He leans on the table and says to Kathy that he needs to clean his teeth.

I have made new covers for the chairs in the sitting-room and curtains to match and Kathy is not pleased. She changes herself dramatically, harshly, but she likes her background to remain the same.

'And look, the cat has ruined one of the covers already'.

It is true! Hundreds of threads have pulled from the flowered material and even as we speak, the cat prowls into the room and caresses itself against my legs. Its hairs cling to my stockings and Kathy curls her lip. She hates the cat. I bought the cat the first time Kathy left home and she came back and felt usurped.

I tell them that we are having lunch in town with Kathy's grandmother and Winchy says he'll sleep for a couple of hours. I show him into Kathy's bedroom, where there are two beds.

'You can use Kathy's bed', I say and I turn back the duvet for him before leaving the room.

'And where do *you* want to sleep?' I ask Kathy.

She just gives me a look without bothering to answer.

'Well, do you like him?' she asks and she eyes me accusingly. She is sprawled out in the bigger armchair, with a second cup of coffee clasped in her hands. She keeps yawning and the sight of her doing that makes me want to yawn myself. I suppress it and my eyes water.

I evade the question by asking how they met.

'At a gig'.

She says no more. I look at her, wondering did she still have her hair then, but I don't dare to ask.

'Are you home to stay?'

She shrugs. 'It depends on Winchy'.

Winchy comes downstairs, rubbing his eyes sulkily. He is too tired to sleep. I give him another coffee.

No one would employ Kathy now. Why, even some of her old friends would shun her. Poddy (who used to play the recorder so badly) wouldn't be seen dead with her nowadays. I met his mother recently and she says that he has really matured in the last couple of years. He has joined a firm of accountants and passed his initial exam the first time round.

Winchy says he works part-time for a recording company.

'Making discs, you know', he says and he winds his index finger round in circles to denote the spinning of a record.

'And how long do you have over here?'

He is just as vague as Kathy. 'I think this is more an area of impulses', and Kathy nods agreement.

There is lots of hot water, so I suggest that they both take a shower to freshen themselves up. They go into the bathroom together and I hear Kathy giggling in that high-pitched infectious way of hers. The shower runs on until they have used up all the hot water in the system. Then it stops. I leave the immersion switched on and decide to say nothing about the waste until I have found out how long they are staying.

Kathy appears after her shower, wearing a multi-coloured multi-striped dress, which seems to be scarcely longer than a tee-shirt. Her legs, admittedly, look beautiful. An even, golden brown from thigh to toe, and her legs too are shaved. Then Winchy appears and I realise that Kathy is really wearing a tee-shirt. A man's tee-shirt, because Winchy is wearing an identical shirt himself, over his jeans. Again I refrain from comment. I consider ringing my mother to cancel lunch, because my nerve is going. But then I realise that cancelling lunch will only raise my mother's curiosity.

Winchy falls asleep in the car as we drive into town and wakes with a jerk as we stop abruptly at the canal traffic lights. He is sitting in the front this time, supposedly viewing the sights and I catch sight of him blinking and making faces to stretch the skin below the eyes. He attempts to take an interest in his surroundings and I point out the Georgian architecture and the onslaught of glass buildings. I even drive in a loop so that he can be shown Trinity College and the Bank of Ireland. Traffic is heavy, and I point them out with a quickly gesturing hand and leave him to work out which is which. Kathy is silent in the back of the car, and when I look into the mirror, I see that she too has fallen asleep. Her head looks so naked, like that of an outsized baby. The sight of it makes me shudder and I look quickly back into the traffic before I lose concentration.

I have a reserved parking space beneath our office block, towards which I am heading. I am a secretary. Well, they call me a personal assistant, which entitles me to more money, but basically my duties are secretarial. I have taken the day off work to meet Kathy (for which she hasn't even thanked me) and tomorrow will therefore be a heavy day, with a double amount of post, and John, my boss, will be regretting his kindness in having allow me the free time and will have to be pandered to.

My mother almost refuses to join us for lunch. We are late and she is standing outside the restaurant entrance, peering back up the road towards us. Because of her bad eyesight, she doesn't see us until we are close by. She is wearing a hat and thin summer gloves. She carries a handbag which matches her shoes. The accessories are part of a wedding outfit, purchased for the wedding of another grand-daughter, two years back. She likes to dress up when she comes to town.

She takes one look at Kathy and her faces registers horror.

'What have you done with your hair?' she shrieks above the surging noise of traffic.

'I sold it', Kathy shrieks back. She bends over to kiss her grandmother on both cheeks, French style, and the tee-shirt rides up to her pants.

Now that I hear my mother's question, it sounds quite normal and I wonder why on earth I didn't ask it myself.

'It's beginning to grow again', I venture and Kathy rubs at her head with a hand. I am feeling relieved. I had been afraid of some involvement with a religious sect.

Winchy says nothing and waits to be introduced. When Kathy does so, he holds my mother's hand a long time in his and he looks into her eyes. He says that he never knew either of his grandmothers. Both died before his birth. 'I feel a great emotional lack'.

My mother extracts her hand and says that we must eat. We have a table reserved and we are already late.

'She looks as though she's been through a delousing station', my mother hisses at me as we walk to the table. The waitress makes a bit of a fuss about the extra place but my mother threatens to call the manager and the waitress subsides. Children at the next table start giggling and pointing at Kathy's hair. My mother quells them too.

It transpires during lunch that Winchy's part-time work is really more on the lines of casual labour. He is not on the payroll but is called upon during busy periods. There are plastic flowers at each table and someone has held a cigarette to the bunch at our table, so that one of the flowers has melted into a lumpy knot of plastic.

'I may go to the States myself', Kathy says. She is eating a beef-burger and tomato ketchup has squeezed out from the side of her mouth and is running into the white, luminous makeup. 'Winchy says he can get me a job on radio announcements. He says Americans go wild for my sort of voice. They find it cultured'.

My mother sighs with irritation and she passes Kathy a tissue from her handbag. 'You are so unrealistic, Kathy. I saw, as I was walking down Grafton Street, a group of street mimers. They wore makeup just like your makeup, but even they looked better. They had a hairline at which the makeup was able to terminate. And besides they had a reason to look odd'.

I know what she is thinking. She is thinking that I have made a thorough mess of bringing up my daughter. She may be right. But why does she also have to think that she would have done a much better job herself? Simply because she brought me up. Kathy is not like me. Kathy, for instance, can't be shamed. Nor can she be bullied. She can only be left alone to rectify her own mistakes.

I push at my mother's leg beneath the table and she looks at me. I frown and shake my head fractionally. Kathy sees the movement and she bursts out laughing.

'Nothing changes', she says and she picks up a chip in her fingers and pushes it into her mouth. She chews on the chip and goes on laughing. 'Don't you love them, Winchy?' she asks, tickling his ear with her greasy fingers. 'Didn't I tell you how they would be?'

'It's what radiates from inside that is so important', Winchy says and he hunches up his shoulder to wipe away her hand. 'Not the outward appearance. Kathy', he says to my mother, 'has reduced herself to the essentials. I think it is very beautiful to have done that. Courageous'.

'When is she going to meet Patrick?' my mother asks and I could kill her on the spot. She must know what she is doing.

Kathy looks at me sharply. 'Who is Patrick?'

'Oh, hasn't she been told about Patrick yet?' My mother looks genuinely surprised but I can't believe that she is. She is quite capable of spite. She probably asked the question to retaliate for being subjected to such a lunch.

Kathy looks at me sharply. 'Who is Patrick?'

Why should I be afraid to tell her and why should my heart begin to race nervously? After all, Kathy should be happy for me. 'Actually, he prefers to be called Paddy', I say. (My mother knows this too, but she disapproves.) 'Paddy is a friend of mine. Very close. We are thinking of getting married'.

The music in the restaurant is too loud and I seem to be shouting the words. I smile at my daughter, who stares back at me from shadowy eyes. The depth of her eyes is exaggerated by the surrounding paint and the lack of hair. I am furious with my mother who is now sitting back in her chair, drinking her coffee and trying to catch the eye of the waitress for the bill.

'I didn't mean to tell you so abruptly', I say to Kathy.

I didn't mean to tell her at all. I had meant to let the situation grow on her. There is no point in confronting Kathy with new ideas. She is automatically hostile to any change. She always has been. She needs to be eased in gradually to new ventures in such a way that they seem almost natural.

Kathy shrugs and turns to Winchy who is smiling politely, unsure whether or not he should congratulate me, unable to understand the nuances, half-asleep. My mother is pulling on her gloves. Now that the damage has been done, she is ready to leave. She is slightly ashamed and insists on paying the entire bill.

'You'll love Patrick', she insists hypocritically as she kisses Kathy goodbye.

We go home and Kathy sulks for the rest of the afternoon, so that Winchy and I are left to attempt conversation together. He is taken aback by Kathy's behaviour, but they are obviously not close enough for him to imagine that he can interfere. She lies on the sofa with her feet on his knees and her back to the edge. She is reading a book and the pages turn regularly and ostentatiously.

Finally, I ask her straight out what she thinks of my intended marriage. Having stayed silent for so long, she can't bring herself to say something nice. Without bothering to roll over, she says she hopes I know what I'm doing. 'You can't have known Patrick that long'.

'Paddy', I murmur. 'He really does prefer to be called Paddy'.

'But I haven't even met him', she replies coldly and the one free shoulder shrugs.

I get to my feet and walk across the room towards the adjoining kitchen. The cat rushes ahead, tail up, hoping for food.

I find myself wishing uncharitably that Kathy would leave for good and not keep coming back. I mean, I love Kathy, but she is too old for the relationship she keeps trying to return to.

'Of course', I call out with cruelty from the kitchen, 'I will be selling the house'.

There is silence from next door. I don't know what I expected. Vociferous rage perhaps? Kathy is too possessive. She thinks she has absolute rights in my house. She can't bring herself to shift her centre of being away from me. She does things to shock me, just to check the integrity of my love. My mother says it is my own fault. She says that our relationship was unnaturally close when Kathy was a child. In particular, she says that

I wouldn't let anyone else come close to Kathy and that now I am reaping the whirlwind of my greed.

I pour myself a glass of orange juice from the fridge and drink it so quickly my teeth ache. Then I return to the other room. Kathy has retreated to Winchy. She has buried her head in his shoulder and though I can't see her face, I know she is crying. He winks one of his small eyes and gestures for me to go away. He imagines he can handle Kathy alone.

I say I am going for a walk and I go out to a call box and phone Paddy.

'Paddy', I say and my voice is trembling.

'She's home?' he asks. I nod at the telephone and then I say yes, she has come and I ask him not to call around until after the weekend. Then I hang up.

Gabrielle Warnock was born in West Cork and now lives in Kinvara. Twelve of her stories appeared in New Irish Writing in the *Irish Press* and she won a Hennessy Award in 1981 for a story published there. Her publications include *Fly in a Web* (Poolbeg Press, 1984), *The Silk Weaver* (Trident Press, 1998) and *Face to Face* (Trident Press, 2000).

Hedy Gibbons Lynott

VINCENT: 'AUVERS'

Their backs bent, cobalt,
Hands that dig and weave,
The loom a trap for light.

Give me

a yellow house
a plain straw chair
no homeless café filled
with starry night,
peach trees in blossom drowning
limpid air.

Your brush spews sulphur
strokes high fields of gold
turns sky into iris,
iris into sky.

You lard on colour with
your knife that I
may feel it with your eyes and
smell it with your skin and
eat it as your last supper.

Rendezvous

Today, it is the girl in the pale pink kimono,
stillness in her dark hair and porcelain skin
who places the tea-tray before her.

She sips green tea from a yellow bowl, grateful
for the shade of cedars
a rustle of maples in the warm breeze
the curl of water from stone
to gold-flecked stone.

A blue-jay shimmers
against creamy spikes of bamboo
Temple-bells chime
across the hazy afternoon
her future in the crumbs of fortune cookies.

She pours more tea from celadon.
He must come.
Soon.

In the brief white silence
when his body curves to her sweetness
her breath rises in a sky of blue-jays,
through the blue of cedar, the amber of maple.

It cradles us, the womb of our history,
this warm kitchen. You, aproned mystery
wave floury arms, blue eyes searching recipes.

Small hands cut and clip brown paper as we make
frilled 'gowns' and 'petticoats' for the tins that take
the mix of love and skill you call a Christmas cake.

Soft plop of butter as you flick the wooden spoon,
fluff eggs, sift clouds of flour, chew raisins, croon
'Silent Night'. A waft of spice fills the room.

You heft fruit, splash grog, slowly fold the mixture:
arm curving tenderly, wrist sensing the texture
of cherries, hunger, almonds, loss, sultanas, pleasure.

Hedy Gibbons Lynott has been writing since retirement, trying to find a voice for her new stage in life. Her work has been broadcast on RTÉ Radio's Sunday Miscellany and Lyric FM's Quiet Quarter, and anthologised in *Sunday Miscellany 2003-2004*. Her poem 'Vincent: Auvers' was broadcast by RTÉ Radio 1 on Rattlebag, as part of a commemorative programme on Van Gogh. Her poem 'Christmas Making' won 2nd prize in the Writelink International Poetry Competition 2001, and was a runner up on Lyric FM's 'A Musical Christmas' competition.

Claire Dagger

I N-AM 'S I DTRÁTH

Amach ó bhéal an droichid traenaigh tháinig ceannsoilse na gcarr ina sruth líomhar, ag fágáil na hoscailte duibhe taobh thiar dóibh. Na ráillí iarainn os a cionn ag roinnt na comharsanachta ina cheantar agus ina alltair. Tagtar ar limistéir fhosctha mar seo gan coinne, thart ar choirnéal, ag bun lána caoil, scaití, ar thaobh eile de dhroichead.

Múchadh fuaimeanna an fhobhaile sa chómhgaracht anseo. Ba chosúil le doras é, béal an droichid, doras éalaithe, ó dhomhan amháin go domhan difriúil; chun an bealach ar ais a aimsiú; bealach ar ais go lampaí ola, coinnle adhanta agus an paidrín páirteach chun an coinneal bhádhadh a athlasadh.

Ba bhóithrín cúng é, taobhaithe ag ballaí cloiche ísle, iarsmaí de ghréasán ballaí a sní a mbealaigh soir trasna an cheantair mar fhigheachán leis na cianta cairbreacha. Ba sheanchosán cairte é síos go dtí an gcladach. D'imir na ceannsoilse ar dhubh agus bhán na gcloch sa dorchradas ag cliseadh na béithigh as a gcodhladh le gileacht na soilse tobainne, ag cur meascán mearaí orthu, a súile móra donna ag caochadh súl go gasta.

Ba oíche fheannaideach Aibreáin í. Bhí na carranna pairceáilte ar fud fad a chéile ar an gcladach. Sheas daoine ina ngrúpaí beaga, cluthartha go maith i gcoinne fuacht na hoíche, glincín á ól ar chúl láimhe. Bhí idir óg 'is aosta bailithe inár dteannta. Thangamar le chéile chun aiséirí Chríost a chomóradh, lá Cásca, ag spéartha lae, ar an gcladach.

Cléireach nua-tagtha don pharóiste a bhí freagrach as an ócáid neamhchoinbhinsiúil seo. Cléireach nua-oirnithe a seoladh chugainn. Bhí lasair na díograise ina ghuth mar a labhair sé linn ón altóir. Lasair nach bhfaca pobal Dé sa séipéal seo le fada an lá gur spreagadh dóchas dearmadta in iomaí croíthe. B'iarracht í filleadh ar ais ar fhréamhacha Ceilteacha na luath-eaglaise. B'iarracht í an seanchreideamh díograiseach a mhúscailt athuair. B'iarracht í an ceangal leis an dúlra a spreag na luath-mhanaigh a adhaint arís i gcroíthe Chríostaithe, a mínigh sé dúinn.

Ba shoiléir ón slua mór a bhí bailithe ar an gcladach gur mhúscail an cléireach óg mian ionainn uilig an seanchosán a aimsiú arís agus folús spioradála ar gcroíthe a líonadh. B'eisean a roghnaigh an cladach, aghaidh ar an muir, le fáiltiú roimh ais-éirí Chríost a chomóradh. Ba é ceann feadhna na gluaiseachta seo.

Mhothaíos an scleondar i manrán chaint na cuallachta thart orm. Is áit draíochta í, an cladach i ndiamhaireacht na hoíche. Do chorraigh an fhuil ionam - le banrán na mara ina toraíocht síoraí ag tuilleadh is ag trá, cuimhne gealaí dúinn ar chruinnmheá imtharraingteacht na cruinne, cuisle na dáimhe thart orainn.

Anseo, leis an ré chaol ag stealladh a scáthanna laige orainn mothaíos macalla don sean saol ar an gcladach fadó, ag bailiú feamna, í spréite amach ar na carraigeacha le triomiú 'is le díol ina gcliminí, báid bheaga ag tógáil caorach isteach 'is amach ón inis. Gach ré sholais, ag lag trá, théadh corr-chapall amach le meilt, tuiscint dúchasacht acu faoin bhfeall taoide idir anseo is ansiúd. Ba chleachtadh targaide é an t-oileán ag fórsaí míleata in aimsir na daoirse. Meall íseal claonta dubh anois é, cur bán na farraige amháin ag tabhairt imlíne dá chrutha.

In fhios nó i ngan fhios, roghnaigh an sagairt óg nua-oirnithe áit an-oiriúnach don cheiliúradh seo. Is learscáil beo é an alltair beag seo do stair na hÉireann i rith an tsaoil bhriste. Lastall, tá fothraigh do dhá thigín ó aimsir an ghorta mhóir. Maireann sliocht na dtionóntaí, a d'oibrigh uair don chinseal sa teach mór, fosta sna tithe nua-aimsire ar an mbóithrín. Tá an teach mór féin ina fothrach le fada an lá.

Is teach scéalach é, an teach ceann tuí sin thall, a sheasann píosa siar ón mbóithrín. Ba ann a fuair saighdiúirí Éireannacha, feisteas na hoíche agus iad ar a mbealach ó Mhuigheo go Loch Garmáin chun páirt a glacadh in éirí amach na bliana 1798. Isteach cosán an trá a tháinig said. Solas i bhfuinneog an áiléir a tharraing a n-aird ar an teach. Tásc ná tuairisc níl le fáil in aon leabhar staire don teach scéalach seo agus an pháirt aon-oíche a ghlac sé san éirí amach cinniúnach sin. Siar, seasann an dún deargánach fós, an clós síonchaite a mhacallaigh uair le coischéim thomhaiste an tsaighdiúra ciúin anois. Bhí dlúth agus inneach na beatha tríd na cianta feicéalach thart orainn.

Pící nó gunnaí ní raibh i bhfolach againne. A mhalairt d'oilithreacht a bhí romhainn an oíche seo.

Anois is arís scoilt fuaim dhíchuibheaneasach an mhiocrafóin isteach ar bhodhrán na mara. Le hais na sceacha geala, a bhí feiceálach leis a mbláthanna bána bláfar i saol na scál seo, bhí thart ar tríocha cathaoireacha plaisteacha leagtha amach i leath-chiorcal. Ós a gcomhair sin bhí tábla beag clúdaithe le héadach bán altóra, dhá chloch leagtha air ar eagla a ghoideadh ag an ngaoth. Taibhseacht ná saibhreas ní raibh le feiceáil. Ní raibh tásc ná tuairisc de chailís órga, coinnleoirí snasta ná coinnle móra téagartha. Ar iarraidh freisin bhí boladh meisciúil na túise agus an mhiorr. Ina n-áit bhí boladh tais an duillúir agus blas na sáile ar an ngaoth.

An mar seo a bhí sé in aimsir an fhill? Nuair a chruinnigh pobal Dé faoi rún thart ar charraig Aifrinn ag spéartha lae nó i nduibheagan na hoíche. Nuair a mhair teachtaire Dé ar theitheadh ar eagla i gcónaí go ndéanfadh scéala air leis an namhaid. Tháinig scáthanna an chaite chun solais arís sa leath-sholas anseo.

Beirt mhairnéalach gallda faoin gcré lastall - fritheadh a gcorp ar an trá in imchéin. Cuireadh anseo iad san áit a bhfuil na táblaí cloiche inniu. Ní deirtear go baileach ar fritheadh beo nó marbh iad; nó ar buaileadh sa chloigeann iad le cloch throm ón gcladach nuair a bhain a gcosa talamh thirim amach; ar sciúrslíodh iad? Ar baineadh a n-éadaí díobh? Ar goideadh uathu pé ní luachmhar a bhí acu sular scaobadh an chré neamhchoiscrithe thart orthu?

Ní raibh boladh dreoite fanta inár ngabhar; ach bhí boladh na sáile im phollaire, a blas ar mo bheola agus taise an fhéir faoi mo chosa.

Bhí tarraingt meallta an dúlra thart orainn. Mar a chruinnigh na págánaigh sa chian aois chruinníomar, ag fanacht agus ag faire amach le haiséirí na gréine agus filleadh an tsolais. Iarsmaí de ghallán chloch ní raibh thart orainn. Níor iobraíodh aon chroí do dhia gallada na fola, *Quetzolcóatl.* Ceiliúradh a bhí romhainn do Mhac Dé Bhí. Mar sin féin, phreab mo chuisle phágánta in oirchill fhilleadh na gréine mar a d'at an fharraige agus mhéadaigh an gála. Sa nóiméad caol díreach sin mhothaíos an slabhra daonna siar. Thuigeas gur sheas mé san áit cheannan céana is a sheas áitreabaigh na háite tríd na cianta, ag táthú gach eispéiris daonna in aon sruth chuisleach amháin.

Bhí an comhluadar ina suí anois ar na cathaoireacha plaisteacha, corr fhearr anseo is ansiúd ina seasamh, na fir céanna is dóigh a sheasann i bpóirse an séipéil gach Domhnach, drogall orthu bheith ina suí, réidh i gcónaí imeacht as.

Rith banrán buartha fríd an slua. D'fhéach daoine anseo 'is ansiúd ar a gcloigín. Dhírigh siad a n-aird ansin ar an mbóithrín ag faire amach do shoilsí charr an tsagairt nach raibh tagtha fós. Mhothaíos mí-dhe ag séideadh inár dtreo.

Bhí aird na cuallachta bailithe dírithe anois ar an spéir le faitíos, tuiscint dhúchasach ionann uilig nach fada go sáródh an lá ar an oíche. D'fhógair an spéir faoileánnach go raibh sé ag láchaint. Ní féidir greim a fháil ar an nóimead aduain sin, an teorann a scarann an oíche 'is an lá óna chéile, an buaicphointe sin nuair a bhrúnn an lá siar an oíche. Cá bhfios ach gur cath síoraí é, cath a throidtear arís is arís i ndiamhaireacht gach oíche.

De dhoirte dhairte bhí sé ina lá. D'éirigh na héanlaithe in airde ar anáil na gaoithe ina ndamhsa deasghnáthach féin, ag faireadh fáilte roimh an solas arís. Is riarach gach dúil dá Dia.

Cuireadh beaguchtach ar an gcomhluadar bailithe. Ainneoin an tsúil a bhí againn uile páirt shiombalach a ghlacadh i gcomóradh ais-éirí Chríost. Níor rollamar siar an charraigh dá uaigh. Níor fhuasclaíomar óna ghéibheann É. Fágadh an abhlann gan coisreacan. D'aiséirigh Dia na nDúl, rí neimhe agus talún, an mhaidin sin gan cuidiú gan cúnamh ó chré an duine.

Céard faoi teachtaire Dé? An sagart nua-oirnithe a mhúscail athuair lasair an chreidimh ionann. An créatúir bocht! Chodail sé istigh. Theip an cloigín air. Nach minic a bhíonns an cholainn claon. Sin mar atá.

Bhí sé ina lá nuair a tháinig sé. Ceiliúradh céad aifreann na Cásca ar an gcladach sa leath-sholas tais; lá ceomhar báistí geallta. Ba shaobh-cheiliúradh é. D'éalaigh uainn an nóiméad leochailleach. Coinbhéirseacht níor tharla.

Sheas mé tóin le gaoth, cac madraí smeartha ar mo bhróg.

Is scríbhneoir dhá theangach í **Claire Lyons Dagger**. I mBaile Átha Cliath ó dhúchas í ach tá curtha fuithi i nGaillimh anois. Cnuasach Filíochta: *Damhsna na nDuilleog*, 2000, *Thar an gClaí Teorainn*, 2004. Úrscéal do dhéagóirí; *An Phluais Ama* 1999, *Filleann an Deamhan* 2001; Duaiseanna: Duais an Oireachtais 2000, An Phluais Ama: Rúin dráma 1998: Duais filíochta, Féile na Samhna, 2004 Deontais ón gComhairle Ealaíne 2001 agus 2002. Breaking the Skin, 2002. Ábhair eile foilsithe sna hirisí eagsúla *Ireland's Own, Comhar, Feasta, Éigse Éireann, Salmon, The Works, Agus, The Burning Bush,* agus ar an radió, Sunday Miscellany agus Thought for the Day.

Breid Sibley

An Oasis in Galway

Under a tree
By the River Corrib
The scent of mint
Wafts towards me.
I think of Minthe
Nymph beloved of Pluto
Whom Persephone changed
Into this plant

The wind rearranged my hair
The tortoise shells
Alight on the valerian
Reaching out from the crevices
Its measured root in water
Brings sleep

I taste a strawberry
And close my eyes and hear
The water over
The grey stones
Two notes from a bird
A child's voice
Distant traffic
I resist moving

Haiku while walking in Tinahely

Evening walk
Ancient fiddleheads uncurl
On the footpath

On the mountainside
Robin, wings fluttering
In the prickly gorse

Magpies nesting
Co-existing
With blue tits

In the woodland
Dipper poised on old log
Dives for larvae

TIME WARP

The south westerly
Catches me at the weir bridge
It twists the shopping bag
Tighter on my wrist
Twirls me first clockwise,
Then counter clockwise
I teeter

I'm transported by the beat
Of Hard Dance, Hard Trance
To high summer in Boston,
The house jumps and expands
With the boom

I am back twenty five years
Driving my sons to the zoo
At Franklin Park
Young men in soft tops drive by
Cars shaking and vibrating with the beat

I do not lose my balance in the wind

The place of stones
is my home
Three goldfinches
sing in the rowan tree
The bees zig-zag from violet
to periwinkle aubretia
The cat watches
and swats the biggest one

The stones and earth in my garden
hold their memories
Cowslips, daisies, corn flowers
forget-me-nots blossom
before the grass is cut
My bones remember ...

The candlelight flutters
Cowslips in a Persian vase
Mozart's Clarinet Concerto
In A major
Where we left off ...
We will resume again ...

A knock on the door
A boy: 'Will you buy a line'.
No, not this time

Breid Sibley lives in Loughrea. She has been a prize winner in the Baffle competition there, and has been shortlisted several times for the Baffle Festival. She was a prize winner in the Cathal Buí poetry competition, and has been published in *Ropes, Crannóg, Galway Now, Westword,* Poetry on the Bus Project and *Time Haiku.* She is working on a novel, provisionally entitled *Audie.*

Mary Ryan

FIRST SEPARATION

Pitch black creates worry worms
that eat my stomach from outside in.
They wriggle into my gut
making me irrational
creating vicious circles.

Will you miss me?
Want my cuddles in the middle of the night?
Will he be as diligent a parent as I?
Watch your step?
Wash your teeth?

I lie in the dark
and curse motherhood
for making me love you
more than I love myself

PARENTAL FEARS

Two days after the funeral
she found his young pyjamas.
Like a smoker about to quit
she dragged in his last smell.

Now each night
I bend low over you,
smell your smell,
feel your skin and hair,
and inhale you into my very soul.

Forgotten moments
revisit as I wait for you in Bewley's.
The days when a smile cured all
smoothing away the fears,
the terrors and the tensions.

Now they are murkied by kitchen wars.

Our love hasn't changed
but is buried beneath mounds
of conditioning.

Can we recapture those moments
of intense communication?
The feeling that we'd invented love,
that ours was different?

Alas, we have once again joined
the queues of desperate people
now sadder and wiser,
sure that happiness is
not found outside oneself
until the next time
we fall in love.

They cross the bridge twice daily.
Belching.
Farting.
Nose-picking.
Ear-rubbing.
Head-scratching.
Each with her thoughts inside a tight head
locked away out of harm's reach.

What goes on
after the curtains are drawn
and the lamps lighted?

Heads tighten to contain the fantasies not to be lived.
They smack them down
go to the pub
jog in the park
watch TV
to jerk themselves back from the edge.

Mary Ryan was born and educated in Galway. She holds a BA and HDE from UCG and an MA in Equality Studies from UCD. Her MA thesis was on Education during Third Age (retirement) and from then her interest in the potential that older peoples' life experience offer to society, has increased. She teaches in Castleknock Community College and has co-ordinated intergenerational projects such as Grandparents' Day in the school. She co-edited Ireland's first third age anthology *No Shoes in Summer* (Wolfhound, 1995) which won the Schools Category of the Living Dublin Guinness Awards, and organised Ireland's first Third Age film festival entitled 'Golden Reels'. Her ambition is to end her professional days in this area. She is currently editing a major anthology of older women's life experiences for Arlen House.

Ginny Sullivan

SUMMER GRASS

I do not know why the hawk's wing,
with its feathery patterns of light and dark,
should overspan that painting of the garden
like God's canopy.
I do not know why
the repetition of the wing
should alight on the canvas
like a fleeting benediction.

The cherry blossoms line up
like soft white sentinels
across the monochrome landscape,
and their limpid forms
are gentle reminders of the spring,
of the subtle beauty
of opaque porcelain
when it contains the palest of liquid.
Between them the table sits solidly
more like an altar on the mown grass
than a place for picnicking.
And in the centre is the rolled drying bale
that marks summers ending.
We know how those men, so far from home,
would lie back in that grass
and watch the hawks fly free.

WILD DREAMS IN THE COROMANDEL

While you were having wild dreams,
your head nested in sand
and your body long amidst the sand-hill grasses,
I knew that I had cast adrift
to see where I would steer,
what currents and waves might take me
over the dark threshold into the light.

And though for you my path seemed hard,
my energy drained, my destination never reached,
to me it seemed I floated
out onto the golden bay,
blown by my own breath,
guided by my own compass,
mooring alongside my birthright.

MERCURY

I am finding, gradually,
the pieces that tell me about you,
so that I feel I can hold you
for seconds in my fingers
like mercury before it slips away,
ungraspable.

The mystery of you
captivates my imagination
and is as unassailable as my longing
which wracks me,
wave-like,
and drowns the known world.

I live with this open heart
and the winds that blow in
rage and chill my centre,
but love flows back and fills the void,
a warm tide lapping around my shores.

Ginny Sullivan is a native of New Zealand who wrote and
published poetry in her twenties and then had an inter-
regnum while her children were growing. She started to write
again five years ago and lived in Galway during 2004.

DESPERATION

What a fool, she thought, looking into the mirror. She ran her fingers over her face. She had everything to live for, and yet when she saw her own image, she no longer recognised herself.

She had taken the day off work and intended to make the best of it. She waved to her neighbour as she pulled out of the driveway. Now there was a woman who was always smiling, always in good humour, not to be met on a bad day because of her cheerfulness.

Ellen always wanted to be left alone when she was in bad form. In fact, she liked nothing better than to curl up in a cosy bed to cry, read or stuff herself with chocolates. It made her laugh afterwards because it was such a waste of time, time that could be used for solving problems, taking long walks on the beautiful beaches nearby. Since the birth of her daughter, of course, this luxury of spending the day in bed was not one she could indulge in.

'Why are you crying Mammy?' was a difficult question to answer. A three-year-old wouldn't understand that a grown-up woman, who on the surface had a lot more in life than others, could feel like a nobody. It was a feeling that was hard to describe even to herself. The depths of this depression were frightening, yet the heights of her happiness were fantastic, and everyone who knew Ellen wanted to be around her at those times. It always angered her that these very people suddenly were busy if she wasn't up to laughing or telling jokes or doing something wild, something daring that would be talked about for weeks.

Ellen was always the court jester, a role she created carefully for herself over the years, but one that now bound her like a cage.

Her life was comfortable enough - nice house, beautiful daughter, a hunky husband and a job - no, a career, that most of her friends envied. Yet, there was something missing and she could not exactly pin it down. That was the frustration, not knowing yourself. She knew it was desperate, that nobody could help her, because she didn't know herself.

Close friends often accused her of living in the past and in the future, but never in the present. She loved nothing more than remembering old times over a few drinks in front of the fire, or, much later, when the alcohol had taken effect, talking about plans for the future.

Ellen was going to master the world - somehow. She never knew how, but nobody cared. It made good conversation. It was nights like these that made people flock to Ellen's home, the house that now seemed empty. There she went again, thinking about the past, when she was still young and still naïve enough to think that the world was waiting for her to leave her mark.

She had left her child with the minder, had taken the day off work so she could think. Her husband told her she did too much thinking. Ellen would have to agree with him, but she couldn't help how she was made. She envied him his carefree attitude to life, to everything. He enjoyed life for what it was, for what it offered him. If he got more out of it he was grateful, but if he didn't he was never disappointed, because he never expected anything to begin with.

But it was more than pure discontent on her part. There was that recent blunder at work. Ten years of work behind her and there was no excuse for her mistake. It hurt her professional pride to think that she had made the error, and being female made it worse.

She had always strived to prove herself, and it always ended up that she worked harder, so she was always a step ahead. As time went by it seemed it was getting harder. She basically couldn't cope, but being a woman she wasn't going to admit that to her male boss. It wasn't that she didn't like men. She preferred to be considered a tomboy than a lady, but the tomboy image didn't tally with the maternal image she was portraying.

The whole thing was a strain. She was disappointed that she was so weak, so weak that she couldn't mix the two images, the two lives. She didn't want to give up her job and she knew that she would be bored out of her brain at home all day every day.

Though she welcomed motherhood, loved her child and looked forward to seeing her grow up, she often suffered from pure loneliness, the kind of loneliness she first experienced when she got married. The feeling that she wanted to run home, the very home that she had escaped from, but which for her would always be home, no matter what. At least she was familiar with it. And it wasn't as if there were problems with her marriage. No, all the problems were within her. If she could put the clock back, she would never grow up. And funny how little girls always want to grow up faster than boys. When they are still toddlers they are putting on their mother's make-up and walking around in high heels. When she was barely a teenager, she passed for someone much older. And then she met her husband. She knew the minute she laid eyes on him that she would marry him, and she was only fifteen at the time. She was decisive and determined that he would leave his long-standing girlfriend for her. He did.

It seemed that all her life she had goals. She wanted him, she got him. She wanted a career, she got it. And she did want suburbia, in a way. She did want to conform. She wanted the burdens of mortgage, bills, responsibilities and dependants. She had them now and she didn't know how to cope with it all. How ironic!

Was life like this for everybody? Did all the young wives and mothers she knew feel like this? Were they putting on brave faces or did they enjoy the strain, or was it a strain at all? Was she simply inadequate? The tears rolled down her face as she drove, aimlessly at this stage. She had intended lodging money in the bank and browsing around the shops.

Though they could be described as a comfortably off couple, there was never enough to splash out extravagantly, like the old days before the baby and the mortgage. She envied people who could walk into a travel agency and book that package holiday or buy that outfit in the shop window, celebrate a birthday with an expensive meal. Of course, any sensible person would tell you that none of these things are necessary to enjoy life, but somehow she craved them simply because she couldn't have them. She was just being childish wanting them. She knew that, but it didn't help her. She had once driven into town with the intention of talking to the Samaritans, but hadn't the courage to go through with it. She felt guilty. She had so much and they would probably look at her with contempt. She didn't need sensible chat anyway. Most of her friends could give her that and they knew her better than a stranger would. Basically, she felt she really had nothing to be depressed about. She just was.

She stopped the car at the prom and got out. The sea was wild at this time of year. She loved standing on the rocks looking out, wondering what life was like on the islands beyond, or beyond that again. What was life like anywhere but here?

But this was it. This was her life, a life that she had structured over the years. She had reached her goal, her plan was complete. And she couldn't see beyond it, she didn't know the next step to take. Childhood talk late in bed at night with her two sisters included the exchange of dreams. Funny how she always had more dreams than they had, had more energy, a *joie de vivre* that people commented on. There wouldn't be enough days in the year for her to do everything she wanted to do; now there were too many hours in the day. They were filled alright. She couldn't be accused of being idle. Her life was hectic, but certainly not fulfilling.

She returned to the car. It had been getting cold standing on the rocky beach. If anyone had seen her, she thought, they would have thought her silly standing there on the beach when the Met. Office had forecast a storm. That was another thing. She always worried about what others thought. As if they cared. She knew she wasn't the centre of everybody's life. She more than likely didn't enter their thoughts as much as she imagined, or would have liked to. That was it really; she loved being the centre of attention. She craved to be a good mother, loving wife and a career woman but she doubted you could have it all.

There was a time when she had never been threatened by anybody. She was the best, the most fun person to be with and what she didn't have in looks she made up for in personality. But what's personality when anyone younger or childless is definitely a threat?

Oh, what the hell. She had to make a decision. She drove off. This indecision had been with her for too long and she couldn't bear it any longer. If she wasn't coping with her responsibilities and everyday life, how could she be of any use to her precious daughter, the apple of her father's eye?

She drove away from the beach, headed into town, and passed by her office, hoping she wouldn't see anyone she recognised. Hoping she would have no reason to stop and talk to anyone.

And before she knew it, she was driving by the docks. She stopped briefly to allow a forklift truck cross the road and she continued on until she reached the end of the pier.

She approached and accelerated until she felt the car float in mid-air, before it hit the water.

Bernie Ní Fhlatharta is a journalist with the *Connacht Tribune* who has contributed to radio and television programmes, locally and nationally. She has also presented programmes for TG4, namely as chat show host for 'Bernie Beo' and 'Thar an Tairseach', where she interviewed Irish speakers living here and abroad. She is married with three children and lives in Moycullen.

Alice Lyons

IN EFFERNAGH

Starched dinner napkins set on the lake
the swans transmit an ur-light I cannot word

its etymology is meant for me. Apologies
to Western Civ, but your myths go in one ear

I can't latch on. Heroics and jokes
won't stick where it counts, mostly.

There *is* something chthonic in this rushy acre,
those purple loosestrife have long-long roots.

My compatriots are on the hoof. The cenotaphs
of Kraków clutter camera memory.

Over in Newgrange why they're packed
like anchovies. Yes, it's best to chuck

what's worn-out. Someone said
Get off the cross, we need the wood!

Unforgettable. And it has to be admitted
Gilgamesh is one beautiful word.

                    …

The rain is to the lake
as your tears to my bowl of palms.
The doddering flight of the cabbage white
is to   is to   is to …

Isn't it just a little like picking up radio Moscow through
your fillings? The ashes
in the hedges wave and promise berries. The only
graffito to be made out reads A LOT

DONE FOR THE BOYS
She said, 'I'm talking to my angels about that one' inside
five minutes of meeting. Not

a good sign.
Yeah it was pretty tight all right but ever try counting the
jabs, the panic medications?

The fillings have stuck since puberty and all that drek. I
once said it was like shaking up a jar of dirt and water;
now I'm not so clear on that.

I held up that grim Pirate Queen shadow puppet and
admired my svelte bicep (tricep?).
Saint Lucy, her gouged eyeballs on stalks (one female,
one black) looks askance:

One eyeball is called *strident*.
The other, *articulate*.

TEDDING

A regular day but it was rowdy
weather. To be honest
it seared the eyeballs. A tear
in the blanket of cloudcover -
light knifed through to one field.
A tractor (it was a Lamborghini)
and mown grass departed
the known world.

I learned a new verb: to ted.

Alice Lyons was born in Paterson, New Jersey and grew up
in the United States. She studied sociolinguistics at The
University of Pennsylvania and painting at Boston
University. In 1998, she moved to Ireland. Her first collection
of poems, *speck*, won the 2002 Patrick Kavanagh Award. In
2004, she received the inaugural bursary from the Ireland
Chair of Poetry Trust. Recent work appears in *Metre, The Irish
Review* and *Poetry Ireland Review*. Her current project in digital
video and 16mm film is a 'film-poem' entitled *Blow-In, County
Roscommon*. She lectures in painting at the Galway-Mayo
Institute of Technology.

Colette Nic Aodha

Ó DIANCÚRAM

Níor mhaith léi admháil ach bhí sí tuirseach. Bhí sí tuirseach de na cuairteanna. Bhí sí tuirseach de na ceisteanna a raibh dualgas uirthi a chur gach uile lá, uaireanta. Bhraith sé chéard a bhí ar siúl an lá úd, nó níos mó ná uair amháin sa lá úd. Nár bitseach ceart í. Cá raibh a comhbhá? Cá raibh a mothúcháin, fiú? Nach mbeadh trua agat do mhadra a bheadh sa chaoi céanna is a bhí sé, gan trácht ar dhuine dá mhuintir féin? Ach bhí trua aici dó agus í ag breathnú air chuile lá, é sínte ar an leaba ar nós marbhán.

Ar a laghad bhí sé fós ann, beo ar éigin. Cúpla seachtain gairid roimhe sin bhí sé amuigh ag obair, chomh sláintiúil le breac. Duine nár ól braon nó nár chaith toitín riamh ina shaol. Rinne sé gach rud dá chlann. Rinne sé gach rud don seisear acu. Fuair a máthair bás agus iad óg. Ní raibh Niamh ach dhá bhliain déag ag an am agus an cúigear eile níos óige ná í. Thuig sí gur bhraith siad uirthi, gur bhraith a hathair uirthi. Ba mháthair óg í dóibh ar fad.

Bhí uirthi foghlaim, bhí uirthi foghlain go h-an sciobtha. Tháinig chuile ní aniar aduaidh uirthi. Thuig sí go raibh siad difriúil mar chlann ag fás aníos gan aon mháthair. Bhí a h-athair difriúil ó na h-athreacha eile a chuala sí faoi. Na h-aithreacha nár ghlac páirt ar bith i saol a gclann. Bhí an-ghrá ag Niamh agus a deirfiúracha agus a deartháireacha dá n-athair. Rinne sé a seacht ndícheall dóibh. Shaothraigh sé airgead agus rinne sé pé rud ab fhéidir leis sa teach tar éis a lae oibre.

Bhí an t-ádh le Niamh gur éirigh go maith leo ar scoil. I dtosach, tar éis báis a máthair, chuaigh na páistí is óige go teach comharsan acu go dtí go dtagadh Niamh abhaile ón scoil. Rinne Niamh an dinnéar don chlann uilig. Chabhradh sí leo lena gceachtanna sular raibh deis aici a ceachtanna féin a dhéanamh. Chuir sí isteach sa bhfolcadán iad chuile oíche. Nuair a tháinig a hathair abhaile bhí dinnéar aici dó. Thug sé cabhair di an teach a ghlanadh nó dá mbíodh tuirse air, bhíodh sé ag rá léi an obair a fhágáil dó agus go ndéanfadh sé féin é an lá dár gcionn. Níor fhág sí aon ní don lá dár gcionn, áfach. B'shin ceacht a d'fhoghlaim sí breá luath ina saol.

Ba mhinic a ghabh a hathair buíochas léi. Ba mhinic a dúirt sé gur *topper* ceart a bhí inti agus go raibh an t-ádh dearg leis go raibh clann álainn aige. Ní raibh trua aige dó féin riamh, ní raibh trua aige dó féin go raibh sé faoi aois a tríocha le seisear páiste agus é ina bhaintreach fir. Níor chaith sé oíche taobh amuigh den teach riamh chomh fada ba chuimhin léi. B'iad a shaol. Ba chuimhin léi na laethanta a chuir sé náprún air féin agus rinne sé císte deas dóibh, go háirithe dá mbeadh sé ina bhreithlá ag éinne acu. Bhí sé iontach maith ag cócaireacht agus ag na deireadh seachtaine ní raibh uirthi dul isteach sa chistin oiread is uair amháin. Chabhraigh sé léi freisin na héadaigh a nigh. Ba obair mhór sin den seachtar acu. Ghabh sí buíochas go minic go raibh éide scoile á chaitheamh ag na gasúir ar scoil, fiú sa bhunscoil.

Bhí sé deacair orthu ar fad dá mbíodh ocáid speisialta ann gan a máthair a bheith i láthair. Bhí sé deacair orthu a bheith cleachtaithe ar an reilig chomh hóg sin. De réir mar a chuaigh na blianta ar aghaidh bhí sé ar nós gur tháinig biseach orthu. D'éirigh siad cleachtaithe ar an saol mar a bhí. Ba dhuine phraiticiúil a n-athair a thuig gur raibh air leanacht ar aghaidh.

Bhí gráin aici ar bharda an dianchúraim. Chuir na beepaí rialta agus gach fothrom ó na hinneal ar fad a bhí ag timpeallú leaba a h-athair isteach go mór ar Niamh. B'fhéidir gurbh é an easpa codladh ba chúis leis. Bhí ar dhuine acu fanacht thar oíche. Cén fáth go raibh uirthi chuile cúram a thógaint uirthi féin? Nach raibh a páistí féin aici anois? Cé go raibh a deirfiúracha agus a deartháireacha fásta aníos bhí siad fós ag braith ar Niamh in am an ngátar. Is dócha go raibh sé nádúrtha go leor ós rud é gurbh ise ba shine. Ach bhí sí tuirseach de. Bhí sí tuirseach ag réiteadh dinnéar na Nollag do gach ball den chlann. Bhí sí tuirseach as a bheith ag cur glaoch ar chuile duine nuair a tháinig an drochscéal.

Níor chóir di a bheith ag gearrán. Bliain ó shin ag dinnéar na Nollag dúirt sí le gach duine nach mbeadh sí ar fáil dóibh fiche ceathair uair in aghaidh an lae, seacht lá na seachtaine, as sin amach mar a bhíodh riamh. Go raibh a saol féin aici leis a gasúir féin agus a céile agus go mbeadh siadsan ag fail tús áite feasta. D'aontaigh chuile duine léi. Duirt chuile duine acu go raibh an ceart ar fad aici agus go mbeadh athrú ar chúrsaí, cinnte. B'fhéidir go mbeadh dinnéar na Nollag i dteach gach éinne acu as sin amach, ag tosú leis an dara duine ba shine sa chlann.

Mhothaigh Niamh i bhfad níos fearr. Shíl sí go raibh athrú suntasach tagtha ina saol. Ach, níor athraigh tada. An chéad bliain eile bhí chuile duine bailithe arís ina teach.

Bhí sé leath tar éis a naoi ar an gcúigiú lá is fichid de mhí Feabhra nuair a fuair sí an glaoch guthán ón ospidéal. Bhí comharsan acu ag obair ann mar bhanaltra agus nuair a tháinig a hathair isteach an oíche sin, chuir sí fios ar Niamh láithreach mar thuig sí ó fear an otharchairr go raibh timpiste tar éis tarlú agus nach mbeadh na póilíní i dteagmháil léi go fóill. Níor thuig Niamh i dtosach cé chomh dona is a bhí cúrsaí. Bhí sé beo agus ní raibh sé gan aithne gan úrlabhra agus an rud ba thábhachtaí, bhí sé san ospidéal cheana féin. Chuir sí fios ar na baill eile den chlann. Dúirt sí leo gan a bheith ró-bhuartha ós rud é go raibh sé fós in ann caint le Deirdre, an comharsan s'acu a bhí ag obair san ospidéal.

Shíl Níamh féin ag an uair nach raibh cúrsaí ró-dhona ach a mhalairt ar fad a bhí fíor, rud ba léir nuair a chonaic sí é fiche nóiméad i ndiaidh sin. Bhí sé sínte sa leaba sa bharda éigeandála agus plúd tinsil thart air. Bhí a aghaidh aitaithe sa chaoi gur ar éigin a bhí sí in ann é a aithint mar nuair a labhair sí leis stáin sé ar ais gan tada a rá. D'iarr sí ar an mbanaltra céard ba chóir di a dhéanamh? D'fhiafraigh sí di cé chomh gortaithe is a bhí sé? Ní dúradh léi ach amháin go raibh siad fós ag déanamh teisteanna air. Níor thaitin an chuma a bhí air le Niamh cé nach raibh mórán eolas aici ar chúrsaí leighis. Chuir sí fios ar chuile duine den chlann. D'iarr sí orthu teacht go dtí an t-ospidéal. Bhí sé ar nós go raibh siad ar buille léi, gur ise a bhí cionntach as an rud a bhí tar éis titim amach. Is beag nár ionsaigh siad í nuair a dúirt sí leo b'fhéidir go raibh rudaí níos measa ná a shíl sí i dtosach. Cén fáth go raibh rudaí níos measa ná a cheap sí i dtosach? Cén fáth nach raibh a fhios aici sin ón tús? Cén fáth nach raibh Niamh ag tiomáint an chairr?

A Dhia na bhfeart, an oíche sin. Go sábhlódh Dia í ó oíche cosúil leis arís go deo. Bhí dea-scéal ann ar dtús, ansin droch scéal, dea-scéal arís agus fíor-dhroch scéal sa deireadh. Bhí sé ag cur fola go h-inmhéanach agus bhí orthu fuil a thabhairt dó. Tuille fola. Bhí cúrsaí ag dul níos measa agus níos measa. Ach bhí a chloigeann ceart go leor. Chuaigh sí abhaile chun cúrsaí a shocrú lena fear céile maidir leis na páistí agus ar uile. Ar ais arís go dtí an ospidéal. Bhí a deartháireacha agus a deirfiúireacha a bhí bailithe thart fén am sin ag gol go fras, droch-scéal eile faighte acu. Ní raibh na dochtúirí in ann stop a chuir leis an cur fola. Ach ní raibh sé fós sa bharda dianchúraim, a smaoinigh Niamh. Shíl sí gur chomhartha maith sin. Rith seisear thairstí agus leaba leo. D'aithin sí an plúd tinsil ach ní dhúirt sí tada leis an dream eile. Ar ball tháinig banaltra amach agus d'iarr sí orthu dul suas go dtí an bharda dianchúraim. Bhí rudaí ag dul in olcas. Bhí siad ina sheasamh i líne taobh amuigh den doras sa bharda dianchúraim. Cuid acu ag gol, cuid acu agus cuma taibhsí orthu, chuile duine ar an imeall.

Cuireadh isteach i seomra feithimh iad tar éis tamall agus tháinig mainlia amach chun labhairt leo. Dúirt sí gur bheag an seans a bhí ag a n-athair ach dá rachadh sé faoi scian go mbeadh seans níos fearr aige. Ní rabhthas in ann stop a chuir leis an bhfuil agus gurb é sin an an t-aon rogha a bhí fágtha acu. Ní bheadh siad dóchasach go mairfidh sé. Bhí sí ag cúartú cead uatha an obráid a dhéanamh. D'fhág sí an píosa páipéar ar an mbord. Bhreathnaigh chuile duine ar Niamh mar ba ghnáth. Sheas sí suas agus shínigh sí an fhoirm. Lig an seomra osna ach bhí an bás fós ag crochadh thart cé nach raibh tú in ann do mhéar a leagan uirthi. Dúirt an mainlia go mbeadh sé faoi scian ar feadh sé uair a chloig ar a laghad agus gurb iad an chéad fiche ceathair uair ba phráinní tar éis sin.

Tháing sé slán tríd an obráid ach bhí sé deacair orthu chuile rud a choinneáil faoi smacht. Bhí a bhrú fola suas agus anuas. Bhí sé fós ag fáil fola agus níor chomhartha maith sin. D'fhan chuile duine acu san ospidéal idir ló agus oíche. Tháinig na banaltraí isteach le tae agus arán rósta ach ní raibh éinne in ann ithe. Níor itheadh greim nó níor óladh braon na laethanta sin. D'fhan cúrsaí amhlaidh ar feadh seachtaine cé go raibh an nuacht níos fearr tar éis cúpla lá ach bhí baol láidir ann go gcaillfí fós é. Bhí an baol ag laghdú lá i ndiaidh lae ach fós féin bhí sé ann sa cúlra ag bagairt anuas orthu. Bhí gach lá ar nós míosa agus iad ag feitheamh thuas sa tríú úrlár, áit a bhí an bharda dianchúraim. Ag cur ceisteanna nó ag seachaint ceisteanna, ag freagairt ceisteanna, ag freagairt an fóin, teachtaireachtaí ag teacht tríd, tuille á gcur. Ní raibh aon éalú. Bhraith chuile duine acu ar Niamh. Níor thuig sí cén fáth, níor mainlia í. Cén fáth ar shíl siad go mbeadh na freagraí uilig aici? Cén fáth ar cheap siad go mbeadh a fhios aici na ceisteanna cuí a chuir? Bhraith siad uirthi mar a bhraith siad uirthi riamh. Ní raibh duine ar bith eile acu. Ní raibh acu ach í. Níor mhaith léi iad a ligint síos.

Chuala sí na scéaltaí faoi tuirse ospidéil. D'fhéadfadh sí na scéaltaí sin a creidiúint anois, mhothaigh sí an domhain mhór ar a gualainn. Mhothaigh sí chuile cnoc, sliabh agus bláth. Na soilse sa bharda, b'iad an ghrian ag taitneamh fiche ceathair uair a chloig, seacht lá in aghaidh na seachtaine. Bhí easpa aer úr ann sa chaoi is a chuirfeadh sé amú sa chloigeann tú leis an tinneas cinn. Lean seachtain i ndiadh seachtaine. Ní raibh cúrsaí ag dul in olcas cé go raibh a n-athair fós gan aithne gan úrlabhra. Dúirt Niamh leo filleadh abhaile toisc go mbeadh orthu dul ar ais ag obair. Ní raibh mórán a d'fhéadfadh éinne a dhéanamh ag an bpointe sin agus bheadh siad in ann teacht ar chuairt ag na deireadh seachtainí. Ag breathnú air agus an aerthóir ag dul isteach agus ag teacht amach as ní raibh an chuma air go dtiocfadh sé chuige féin arís go deo cé nár dhúirt Niamh sin leo. Thóg sí gach cúram uirthi féin mar a thóg si riamh gan gearrán.

Is ar éigin a bhí a páistí féin feicithe aici ó bhí an timpiste ag a hathair. Bhí sí tinn den bhia a dhíol siad i mbialann an ospidéil. Bhí sí tinn de na sceallóga a dhíol siad trasna an bhóthair ón ospidéal. Ní bheadh deis aici dul aon áit ceart chun greim le nithe a fhail. Ní raibh deis aici. Ní bheidh deis aici agus ní bheadh sí sásta an deis a thapú dá dtarlódh sé.

De réir a chéile tháinig feabhas ar a h-athair agus bhí sí in ann dul abhaile thar oíche. Bhí sé gan aithne gan urlabhra chomh fada sin agus nuair a tháinig sé amach as, bhí sé beagáinín seafóideach. Chuir sin olc ar Niamh. B'fhearr léi é a fheiceáil sínte ar an leaba ar nós marbháin ná sa chaoi sin. Bhí sé deacair uirthi. Ní fhaca sí é ar meisce riamh ina saol agus chuir sé isteach go mór uirthi nuair a d'iarr sé uirthi an citeal a chuir thíos agus iad í ina suí in aice lena leaba sa bharda dianchúraim. Nuair a shíl sé nach raibh sí ag déanamh a thola, d'éirigh sé crosta léi. Ní raibh sí in ann é a sheasamh. Níor dhúirt sí tada don dream eile go raibh sé mar sin. D'inis sí an dea-scéal leo i gcónaí. Go raibh sé ag feabhsú agus go raibh sé chuige féin arís agus ag caint léi mar ba ghnáth. Níor dhúirt sí leo gur stráinséir a bhí sa duine ins an leaba. D'aithin sé í ceart go leor ach na rudaí a dúirt sé ...

Chuir sé as di an chaoi a bhreathnaigh sé uirthi uaireanta, gan labhairt. Bhíodh sé ag stánadh uirthi ar nós gealt, a shúile folamh in a chloigeann. Chuir sé faitíos uirthi nuair a bhí sé mar sin. Bhris sé a croí mar ba dhuine cliste, ciallmhara é cúpla seachtain roimhe sin. Níor lean sé ar aghaidh ró-fhada, bhí sí buíoch as sin. Dúirt na dochtúirí nach raibh a leithéid neamh-ghnáthadh. Bhí sé tar éis an méid sin leigheas a chuir trína chorp. Ní fhéadfadh sé a bheith ceart. Bhí sé beo, fós leo, ba chóir di a bheith ag céiliúradh. Ach bhí sé deacair. Bhí sé deacair breathnú ar a chorp briste. Bhí an dea-scéal aici le h-insint don chlann mar a bhí riamh. Bogadh é as an bharda dianchúraim go gnáth bharda. Chuaigh sí ar ais ag obair. Bhí sé níos deacaire ag féachaint air agus ag labhairtt leis agus eisean amhail is nach raibh tuairim aige céard a tharla agus ise breá sásta gan aon tagairt a dhéanamh de ach an oiread. Bhí an méid seafóid a bhí sé ag rá ag laghdú de réir a chéile. Thug sé sin faoiseamh mhór do Niamh. Thosaigh sé ag caint ar chúrsaí sa bhaile. Bhí sé ar ais chuige féin go h-iomlán.

Tháinig an chlann uilig chun cuairt a chuir air ag na deireadh seachtainí. Mhothaigh sí ciontach mura raibh sí ag tabhairt fios air gach aon lá, fiú nuair a raibh na daoine eile thart. Níor labhair siad ar chéard a tharlódh nuair a bheadh sé réidh le teacht abhaile ón ospidéal. Bhí beagnach chuile cnámh ina chorp briste. Thógfadh sé i bhfad air na mion rudaí nach smaoineann tú orthu a dhéanamh dó féin. Bheadh air siúlóid a ath-fhoghlaim. Ní raibh sé in ann é a bheathú é féin. Ach ní raibh sé i bhfad ó shin nuair nach raibh sé in ann aon rud a ithe. Smaoinigh sí cé chomh sásta agus a bhí sí nuair a dúirt an mainlia léi tráthnóna amháin gur féidir léi uachtar reoite a thabhairt dó. Bhí gliondar uirthi. Níor ith sé ach spúnóg amháin ach b'shin an tús.

Bhí sé an-lag go fóill ag an am céanna. Ar ball cuireadh ina suí é ar feadh nóiméid nó dhó gach lá. Ní raibh sé sásta a bheith fágtha ar chor ar bith. Bhraith sé go raibh sé ag titim i gcónaí cé nach raibh sé ag bogadh ar chor ar bith. Chuir seo as do Niamh. Níor mhaith léi nuair a d'iarr sé uirthi a chos a bhogadh dó sa leaba ach an oiread. Bhí cos amháin nach raibh ró-dhona ach bhí an chos eile scriosta ar fad. Dúirt sé léi go raibh sé in ann é a bhogadh leis féin ach bhí amhras uirthi. Bhí sé mar an gcéanna maidir leis an gcos eile. Shílíodh sé go raibh a chos ag titim amach as an leaba agus bhíodh sé ag iarraidh uirthi é a chuir ar ais san áit ceart cé go raibh sé fós san áit chéanna. Mhínigh an banaltra go raibh seo nádúrtha go leor d'othair mar eisean. Uaireanta bhíodh sé ag lorg a cabhair agus ní raibh sí in ann tada a dhéanamh dó nó bheadh faitíos uirthi tada a dhéanamh gan comhairle a fháil ó altra nó dochtúir. Níor thuig sí cén fáth go raibh drogall air glaoch ar na banaltraí. Bhíodh sé ag rá i gcónaí nár mhaith leis cuir isteach orthu agus go raibh tuille le déanamh acu. Go raibh siad ag teastáil níos géire ó na hothair eile. Níor dóigh léi go raibh ach níor dhúirt sí tada.

Dé réir a chéile chuir siad é ina sheasamh. Tar éis sin thóg sé cúpla céim. Níorbh fhada go raibh sé in ann siúl go dtí an leithreas. B'shin an uair a dúradh le Niamh go raibh sé réidh chun dul abhaile. Bhí amhras ar Niamh ach bhí sí sásta ag an am céanna. Bheadh uirlisí speisialta ag teastáil dó a chuideodh leis nuair a bhí sé ina theach féin. Ní bheadh sé in ann aire a thabhairt dó féin. Nuair a chuireadh an cheist air san ospidéal cé a bheadh ann chun aire a thabhairt dó dúirt sé go mbeidh sé in ann aire a thabhairt dó féin. Dúirt Niamh leis gan

a bheith craiceáilte go raibh dóthain sa phota dó ina
teach agus go mbeadh go deo. Sin a bhíodh sé féin ag rá
dá dtiocfadh éinne chun fanacht leis nach raibh súil leo,
go raibh dóthain sa phota agus go mbeadh go deo.

SPEAKING MINORITY LANGUAGES

It was our first encounter
and our last.
Seeing her helpless shape
I went out of my way to praise.

She startled, shocked I knew her name
or maybe that I read
and spoke a minority language
and if I did, was anyway keen on verse.

Taking her frail hand, I didn't shake it
in case it might break,
amazed that great verse emanates
from such a fragile face, body crooked with age.

Greater poets spilled out and in
but I rested all my interest with her
until another eager fan took my place.
Yesterday her words froze on her lips

never reaching her fingers.

SNOW

Powder the page with words
of soft fallings,
white drifting folds,
things iced
like any other
worth their salt.

REFLECTION

On mirror water
Lir's children uptail,
nosedown, looking for roots.
In the background

the cragged leftovers
of a crannóg
bears upright shoots
of no circumference.

I feel a feather-gaze,
meeting it I see
a thousand rings
in the eyes of a swan.

Colette Nic Aodha was born and reared in Shrule, Co. Mayo
and lives in Galway with her three sons. She studied Irish
and history at UCG. A qualified teacher, she works in the
Presentation College, Headford, her old alma mater. Colette
has published three volumes of poetry with Coiscéim, *Baill
Seirce* (1998), *Faoi Chrann Cnó Capaill* (2000) and *Gallúnach-ar-
Rópa* (2003) and one volume of short stories, *Ádh Mór* (2004),
the title story of which won the Foinse short story
competition for August 2004. Her poetry has been
anthologised in *Field Day* and in *The White Page/An Bhileog
Bhán* (Salmon, 1999). Colette's poetry was awarded a prize in
the Dún Laoghaire Poetry Festival in 1993.

Ursula Rani Sarma

The Hindu-West Clare Project

Stunning,
With breaths of lace and threads of gold
I have become
My father's daughter,

At last.
At long last.

Calcutta early morning light,
My brother is searched for bombs, rifles, rashers,
Any remnants of home,
And I,
I watch the lizards run along the window panes
and try not to let the heat of the place,
The sultry peach like beauty of the place,
Run away with me.

Our luggage lost,
I slip inside the sari folds
and try to make them my second skin,
and try to become my father's daughter,

At last.
At long last.

For I want to be an ingredient of him,
A tiny part that will make me a fraction of something,
Someone so perfect and delicate
That he is dead.
And in his death,
Glorified and sanctified.

And so I want my crooked nose to be the same as his.
A link to the divine.

I walk alone ...
Like a lone and dreamful thing that can only keep itself
in dreams as long as it never rests,
Or sleeps,
As long as it searches on,
For its measure is in its searching,
Like a diamond caught in coal black jaws.

I walk alone ...
In the wind on different shores I hear strange voices call
my name in a familiar fashion,
Like friends,
They smile and nod encouragingly,
But don't ask me to stay,
Instead their affection pushes me further on away.

I walk alone ...
And the walk sometimes seems like a Promethean curse
nailed to the small bones of my back,
Like penance,
For being born an unfitting thing,
A coin that will not be slotted through,
Hands that will fit no pair of earthly gloves.

I walk alone ...
Because I am the only one who hears the mottled voices
that breathe and stamp out the rhythm to which I walk,
Beautiful drum beats moving off into the air,
Like children learning to fly.

I walk alone because I am less likely to break through the
skin deep ice that way,

Like a creature on a dew drop,
With tiny feet.

To be returning is like trying to fold a piece of cloth that
is in tatters.
Unformed.
In bits,

And yet trying inevitably to make frayed edges meet
others.

Your garden's apple trees,
Branches like breasts full of milk.
Full of fruit.
To pass on.
To nurture.
To fruitfill.

The day you hung the rope from that slender branch
and made a swing for me.
For my scrawny self.
To sit upon and swing up and down because what did I
have to worry about?
No thing.

When I try now to place you somewhere solid
It's the grainy things that come back.
Blue paisley pyjamas,
Grey stubble,
Coarse cardigans,
Woollen things.
That night,
in the hospital.
Four-ish.
Hospital sounds.
Quiet sedated sleeping geriatrics.
Then
Your eyes,
blue clear and

- Is it you?
- It is.
- Will I stay awake?
- No sleep.
- But won't you be lonely?

I am.
I am so lonely without you.
I am so sad and neglected and unfortunate without you.

Once I dreamt there were banshees in your apple trees,
But I fought them back to the gate posts,
They crept back in and took you while I slept.

ADRIFT

Into bridges of time
Where water was on the same level as
You or I.
I was adrift,
Dreaming of better times
Where sunsets came upon us
Like drops of water in a lake
And we
We had the patent on romance and love
And all sentiments rose coloured -
On hand holding
And drinking from the same glass -

There are days when these times
seem to have drifted continents away in the undertow
and you and I are left
stammering,
staring,
clutching these shining moments to our chests
like drowning things.

PICTURE OF MY FATHER HOLDING ME

You're holding on so tightly
It's as if you're afraid I'll suddenly take flight,
Or be reefed from you in the next instant
By a passing phantom

Your eyes are closed and you're pressing a kiss to my face
Cheek to blood-linked cheek,
It's as if you somehow knew that our embraces
Were to be savoured and worshiped and measured in
moments
My two year old self stares out boldly
Mockingly as if to say
This man will love me for an eternity and back
Just you wait and see

I could not have known,
That within a year
I would be the only one of us left to watch this picture
develop
Or that I would ever be fatherless,
A lone feather on a hurricane beach.
Or that I would spend a lifetime trying to remember,
being held fast in your arms,
Enfolded and wrapped up and adored like a precious
thing,
In a picture,
One I cannot remember,
One I cannot forget.

RECURRING DREAM

On a lake of glass
I sit cross-legged
Barefoot
Fishing
Catching words

I hear my mother humming
Smell the spices deep and fat in the air
Hanging like moving bones
She calls out for me in the voice of a young woman
But I cannot answer

I am fishing
I have caught all the words.

TOLL

When the toll bell rang out,
Eighteen long dead sounds,
The village mourned like a huge animal breathes

In - together
Out - together

This huge belly of grief rising and falling
In a collective exchange of gasses
- stunned -
For what God would rob a town of its children?
What deity would see it fit to do such a miracle as this?
To leave eighteen small coffins ...
Lined up alongside each other ...
Like tiny seals turning their bellies to the sun.

Ursula Rani Sarma is co-founder and Artistic Director of Djinn Productions. She has been Writer in Residence for The National Theatre London, Paines Plough Theatre London and for Galway Local Authorities. Her plays have been staged and have won awards both nationally and internationally. She is currently developing work for the Abbey Theatre, the National Theatre, Paines Plough Theatre, London and the BBC, amongst others. She has just completed her first collection of poetry, is developing work for the screen and is editing a series of her stories for children.

Moya Cannon

FORGETTING TULIPS

Today, on the terrace, he points with his walking-stick
and asks
'What do you call those flowers?'

On holiday in Dublin in the sixties
he bought the original five bulbs for one pound.
He planted and manured them for thirty-five years.
He lifted them, divided them,
stored them on chicken-wire in the shed,
ready for planting in a straight row,
high red and yellow cups -

treasure transported in galleons
from Turkey to Amsterdam, three centuries earlier.
In April they sway now, in a Donegal wind,
above the slim leaves of sleeping carnations.

A man who dug straight drills and picked blackcurrants,
who taught rows of children parts of speech,
tenses and declensions
under a cracked canvas map of the world -
he loved to teach them the story
of Marco Polo and his uncles arriving home,
bedraggled after ten years journeying,
then slashing the linings of their coats
to spill out rubies from Cathay -

today, losing the nouns first,
he stands by his flower bed and asks
'What do you call those flowers?'

The bog is cracked and red-gold
and, where the stream has laid bare
half its stone bed
the quartzite is fluid,
persuaded by the nuances,
the stutterings and inflections,
of the element with which
it has conversed for millennia.

Here, a white streak of quartz interrupts
long, tender slopes of stone,
scoured and scored by pebbles
now nested in dry pools
a descending stream of quernstones,
which grind nothing
but time.

I lie down in a stone bowl
in the sun-warmed streambed,
my head beside the flow,
and let the blethering of mountain water
erode me.

Moya Cannon (Máire Ní Chanainn) was born in
Dunfanaghy, Co. Donegal in 1956 and now lives in Galway.
She studied history and politics at UCD, and International
Relations at Corpus Christi College, Cambridge. She has
published two collections of poems, *Oar*, (Salmon, 1990, 1994;
Gallery, 2000) and *The Parchment Boat* (Gallery, 1997). A third
collection, provisionally entitled *Carrying the Songs* is nearing
completion. She has been an editor of *Poetry Ireland Review*
and has held a number of residencies, most recently at the
Centre Culturel Irlandais, Paris. She has been a recipient of the
Brendan Behan Award and of the Lawrence O'Shaughnessy
Award. She is a member of Aosdána.

Aoife Casby

THE ROBIN

The male robin sings in winter time too. Maybe it sings because it likes singing. The sound of its voice on the cold air. They make up twos, robins do. The female picks the male or so they say. He is the one who is chosen. Both robins sing in summer.

In Anna's back garden, the pair of red-breasts spent a lot of time in the hawthorn tree. The spikes were hard, dark and sharp. Anna woke into the bright cold on this day, the day of the robin. Irish was flying in her head. The dim morning eye of the sun bleared indistinct behind the holey lace curtain. It was crooked and dawn oozed. Cherry in the printed drape was half running in the draught and quiet was at its loudest and you could hear your heart beat against your ribs and if you tried to touch it your bones shivered.

There was sleep in her eyes. Anna sat up rubbing. Delicate yawn and the pink spaces between her tiny teeth watered. Her hair was matted in an uneven mess along her right face. She fell into feet hanging over the edge of the low bed. Another yawn, clear eyes and the carpet was on her foot-skin. Wiry ticklish, she scratched the bottom of herself leaving her ghosts underneath the woolly blankets. Although she could still feel their cool fingers tapping on the pivot in her dirty neck. The squared orange quilt had holes in it. Torn along the fringe. She imagined that from behind she is black. She imagined it, whirling, but it was too early in the day to try a fast turn.

Anna looked for her socks and shoes. Stood in front of the vacant fireplace (because in that room there was a place where fires used to live). She stood where the influence of the wind came and sucked the warm out. The voice of the wind is easy in the chimney like a friend. She let the silence and the emptiness go through her as if she were made from tissue. No one else was awake. Sometimes the birds drop down twigs into the room from the blackness when they try to make their nests. The twigs are always hard, too hard to sleep in. Anna's mother threw out the little mossed branches from the bottom of the bed. They made scrapes on Anna's toes. She wiggled her shoulders into moving and looked about the floor. She couldn't find her socks. Rubbed her lonely shoes with her left toe contemplating the buckled shoes and the lost socks.

A dislocation of spirit. Like she was outside herself and inside herself at the same time but the feeling of being inside was cold. Like walking into an empty room. Like the one she was about to leave. Like walking into the silent outside. Fields with no machines. Walls with no people. Like waking up on a bright cold morning and your breath makes mist. On days like this, her body lost something like heat and the fire she remembered warm seemed to be more dangerous.

Beyond the curtains the birds were noisy. No-one else was awake. Anna closed her eyes and forced her ears. Sometimes she thought she could hear them breathing in the next room and sometimes she knew it was the wind breathing through the cracks around the window. She liked the way the orange from the curtain seeped in behind her closed eyes. Then she opened the door and stepped into the stale living room. Crossed in front of the powdery embers. Inside her she could hear the bird chorus, banging her ear bones. The bigness of Mam and Dad underneath their covers was quiet. She closed their door too and padded back in front of the crumpled fire. To look at herself in the mirror. She had to stand on the heavy arm of the chair and stretch. Her ankle looped a crunch. Anna looks different when the curtains aren't open. Light was heavy in the mirror too. Darkened. The mirror reminded her of spiral staircases. Birds still chirping in her head.

The birdsong turned into 'Ár n-athair atá ar neamh ...' Our Father who art in heaven. Inside her too. Anna was glad that she could remember the first lines.

In the kitchen she dragged a little red and dirty white wobbly stool to the back door. Leaned up and pressed the black lever latch. Opened it. Held the door open with the stool and stepped pyjamaed and barefooted into the yard. She watched goosebumps on her arms and stared at them until their pale blueness was imprecise in her loose eyes. Birds chanted and sang in the hedges and trees. Singing. Singing. Singing. The sun came gold through crystal water on the leaves and branches. Anna walked into the rough garden where the wet grass wept on her cold feet, turning them red. Balanced one footed she saw the dirt on the bottom of herself creased.

Anna made growls in her throat and recognised her tummy noises as hunger. Drifted back to the kitchen thinking about bread and milk. She moved the stool and closed the door on the rising sun. Her small feet tingled now on the ox-blood floor. In the quiet.

Out of the silence, there was a loud crack against the window. Thudded like a heart. A flurried flutter. Fast blurred. Heart racing. Like the ghosts had their fingers around her throat now. Anna stood still. Waiting for the feathers to move again.

She held her breath and the thumping blood rocked her body. Dawn was noisy in her ears again. '... go naofar d'ainm, go dtagadh do ríocht ... go naofar d'ainm, go dtagadh do ríocht ... thy kingdom come'. She could feel her sharp breaths in her hearing and cold at the back of her nose and down her throat. Still she waited.

The robin was quiet for another minute then tried again to batter its way through the clear glass. Anna watched its frenetic efforts for a few immobile moments and in this time, became painfully acquainted with the bird's distress. Through this understanding, calm came back to her. She rubbed the soft velvet at the top of her ear. *Amazed* that the robin came in the open door. So open it!

'It's OK little robin. I'll get you out. Open the door and you can go'. It was a real promise that she made and it jewelled her small voice with hope, so much that her breath sparkled with the intensity of her undertaking. She repeated it. 'It's OK little robin. I'll get you out. I'll get you out'. Whispering a lyrical musical delivery into the cold kitchen.

The robin was on the windowsill. His feathers were not neat now. Anna dragged the red stool back to the door and reached to press down the black shiny latch in a second ritual that morning. All the time whispering to the robin and keeping a watch on him. He tried again to squeeze himself through the window. Batter flutter. The sound of his wings was approaching noiseless.

'Come on now. This way'. She pointed to the open door but the robin did not move.

Anna walked across to the sink pulling up her loose-hipped night clothes. Feet hurt. Had to leave the stool to keep the door open. A small window was slightly ajar, over the large one that never opened and where the robin was trying to escape. He messily crouched in the corner of the sill. Beside the soap. He couldn't see the way out.

'Are you one of the robins that lives in the wall at the thorny tree?' Anna leaned into her soft words. She could almost smell him. The little bird's body shuddered. His eyes sparkled and if she had the word for it, she would have named the light there terror.

'I'll tell your friend that you're here?' Stopped. Looked at the ceiling where there were brown splats. Then she thought better of it. What if his friend came in here too and then *she* got trapped. Anna wanted to cry.

Sat watching the futile efforts of the bird for a few more minutes. 'Have you got babies?' she whispered.

It chirped.

'Oh robin. Please don't sing. Don't sing'. Anna put her forefinger tight vertical across her white tight lips. Shaking her head. 'Please don't sing in here. They'll wake'.

She decided to take the stool away so the back door closed freely, shut on the way out and there was no escape until she could open the little window. The robin made another huge effort to fly at the pane. One wing dangled a little. It twittered, cheeped again. Anna heaved the scratching stool closer to the sink.

'Don't sing robin. Don't. Don't. My daddy shoots pheasants ...'

She stopped, feeling shock stretching on her face.

'Sssh ... he shoots crows too ... and pigeons'. There was a rabbit hanging on the back of the door once. 'Maybe he'll shoot you, so be quiet robin please'. Anna slowly got onto the stool. The robin's flurrying was intense now. 'Ssssh robin. Please. You can sing when you're back in the outside'.

Anna crept closer, hoisting herself up onto the sink. It would be good if she could open the top little window and maybe the robin would find that easier. She kneeled on the ridged draining board like it was a pew leaving lines in the soft skin between the bones. The robin flew at her. She ducked. The robin flew at the fridge. Anna felt a numb sinking inside her. The same as drinking cold orange with ice in the sunshine. It folded down into her middle. Her shoulders dropped and she watched the robin flutter at the fridge and then disappear behind it.

She crawled backwards down to the floor. Back to the door. Opened it again. Waited again. The robin made no other move that she could hear. Finally Anna crept around the fridge. She couldn't see the bird. Anna was really cold now. Head pressed against the wall, she had one eye at the behind of the fridge. It was grimy. In the wire dusted gloom she imagined she saw some feathers. Anna reached in but her arm was not long enough. She tried the sweeping brush but could not see what she was doing. Then she used the brush as a lever and pushed and pushed and pushed. Dropped the handle and grabbed the side of the fridge and jammed her feet against the wall. Pulling. All her tiny Herculean strength and she fell. Clattered against the stool. Anna didn't cry. But the fridge had moved enough for her to reach her hand in. The clamour in her chest, loud.

She felt the yielding feathers and the bird didn't try to get away. Anna removed the lifeless body from behind the fridge. A dislocation of spirit. Like she was outside herself and inside herself at the same time but the feeling of being inside was cold. Like walking into a room empty of life. This one. Like walking into the silent outside. Fields with no machines. Walls with no people. Like waking up on a bright cold morning and your breath makes mist. On days like this, her body loses something and a fire is dangerous.

The robin was dead.

This is the first dead thing Anna has held. This is the first dead thing that Anna has made dead. She held the still warm corpse with its strange heaviness in her hand. Heart wild. Anna stroked the feathers and the red orange unheaving chest with her finger.

'... *go ndéantar do thoil ar an talamh ... thy will be done on earth*', she whispered.

Fright engorged itself on Anna; on her neck, her chest, her middle, right into the kitchen that got bright with tears. Scared that her mammy and daddy would get up and see the killed bird. Deep inside she knew a robin wasn't like a pheasant or a crow. A robin was special.

She decided to bury it.

To have a funeral she would need a coffin. Small. Anna held the bird and went into the living room, to the fire and to the box of cigarettes lain there. With no second thought, like this was a plan coming from a huge yawn inside her, a plan that she knew already, she took the box. She brought it to the sink and wet the cigarettes that lay askew, then emptied the box, took the cigarettes outside and buried them first. In a dry hole that she scraped with her fingers. The sun cleared the side of the trees. There was no sign of the other robin.

In the yard she had a warmth in her cheeks that tingled like her feet and her pyjamas had grey clay along the bottom. Threads hung. She crossed the boundary of the yard and hurried to the trees at the bottom of the field. To a corner in the clearing. There she dug the resting place for the robin. From out of the crumbling dirt. She had a grave-digging twig that was forked. With the twig and her fingers she scooped and scraped a hollow shape-circle for the cigarette box. Bright metal coloured rays came like magic spells through the shaking leaves.

'... *mar a dhéantar ar neamh* ...'. Just like heaven.

Kneeling high, no longer aware of her cold sore feet, Anna pulled out the gold paper carefully from the cigarette box and folded it. Stuffed the dead bird into the space where the cigarettes had been. The red and white box swelled round with its extinct burden. She hummed. Birds chattered in the trees. She spent delicate minutes at her work. Squeezing her thighs together, she needed to go to the toilet. She could feel the urgency in her legs and it brought water into her mouth again. Hunger resumed its elusive nagging in her belly.

'... *ár n-arán laethúil, tabhair dúinn inniu* ...'. Wishing for milk and toast and jam.

She cleaned five little stones and laid them in a circle on top of the clay mound, one, two, three, four, five, then covered it with the golden blanket. Anna picked up her twig again and snapped the dry wood. Made a sort of a cross. Sat hunkered. Waiting. Irish spinning in her head.

'... *and forgive us our trespasses as we forgive those who trespass against us* ...'

She blessed herself. Deliberate. Top. Middle. Left. Right. Her pointed fingers were tight white. Anna wasn't sure if knowing the 'Our Father' would make up for killing the bird.

Aoife Casby is a visual artist and writer living in Carraroe. Her fiction and poetry have been published in *Northwords, Whispers and Shouts, Criterion, The Cork Literary Review* and online in *west 47*. She holds an MA in psychology from UCD.

Hannagh McGinley

INNOCENCE

One day, I'm chasing butterflies, nowhere!
Believing in rainbows, pots of gold
Enjoying all seasons, all of nature
Believing in stories, I myself told.
Back then my imagination was welcomed
I had dreams I knew could come true.
And now, I feel fairly different.
That imagination makes me blue
Because now, I am faced with reality
it interferes with all of my dreams
I am forced to admit, and it breaks my heart
But all is not what it seemed.
Oh I wish I could return
return to innocence!

THE PIT

Give me back those stolen years
wipe away these growing fears
I have risen from the pit
but keep falling back in.
Am I just so weak
I can't reach the top?
Is sadness caving me in?
I feel the boulder bruise my head
the sides are coming too close
suffocating, but I'm trying to breathe
I'm down here, please somebody hear
just give me a hand, I'm too tired to climb

The pit bottom is catching up.

Hannagh McGinley is a student at NUI Galway. In her view, she has to date only written poetry from the heart, but some day she hopes to write from the intellect.

Ann Henning Jocelyn

WATERFALL
a serious comedy in three acts

An excerpt from ACT II, Scene Four.

ROGER, *a mild-mannered accountant approaching fifty, is having grave doubts about his life. His wife, unable to tolerate what she sees as increasingly irrational behaviour, has told him to leave the home. After a six weeks' separation, she gets a message that he has been arrested. She visits him in the holding cell of a police station.*

- - -

LAURA sits down.

Silence.

LAURA:
Roger - I am so sorry.
I've been very selfish.
Very unfair.
I blame myself entirely.

Pause.

I never meant to turn you out of the house.

ROGER:
I would have gone anyway.

LAURA:
I've been expecting you back ever since.

ROGER:
It was only a matter of time.

LAURA:
I do understand.
You wanted some time on your own.
Well you've had it now.
See where it landed you.

Pause.

I should never have let you go.
You were in no fit state to manage on your own.
Perhaps I didn't realize just how frail you are.
Six weeks ... and you've hit rock bottom.
My poor darling.

Pause.

I don't hold anything against you.
Doctor Wilson has explained it all so well.
How your condition affects your judgement.
You can't be held responsible for any of your actions.
Be it women, or anti-social behaviour, or ...
criminal activity.

Pause.

He's going to write a letter to the authorities,
confirming that you're a psychiatric patient under his care.
That way you can't be held legally accountable.
They may not even press charges.
No one will have to know.

Pause.

In fact, I just had a word with the nice Detective Sergeant.
He was very accommodating.
I suppose my position as head teacher was a help.
Apparently, all I have to do is sign a document,
and they'll let you out of here.

Pause.

On condition, of course, that you come home with me.
That you start your treatment and stay with it
until you're well again.

Pause.

Is it really true what Tom told me,
that you've given up your job?

ROGER:
Er ... yes.

LAURA:
Well we'll have to do something about that.
The doctor says it's essential that you stick to your old
routines.
Live exactly as you used to before you got ill.
I'm sure they'll take you back, given the circumstances.
And allow you time off for your therapy sessions.

Pause. She gets up.

Let's go then.

ROGER:
No.

LAURA looks at him.

ROGER:
I'm not coming.

LAURA:
Roger -

ROGER:
I'd rather stay here.

LAURA:
You really are out of your mind.

ROGER:
I have no choice, Laura.
I can't walk backwards.
I have to move forward.
Where my vision takes me.

Pause. Laura sits down again.

LAURA:
(*taking his hands*) My dearest.
You had everything.
A good job, more than enough money,
nice friends, a comfortable home ...
A beautiful daughter and a wife who,
strange as it may seem, still loves you dearly.
You're on the brink now of losing it all for ever.
I'm offering to bring you back.
You can't afford to refuse.

Pause.

ROGER:
You know the old rose bush growing at the bottom of
the garden?
The one we never bothered to prune?
Have you looked at it lately?
Have you seen what a mess it's become?
All leggy, overgrown, full of suckers.
It doesn't carry blossom any more.
In fact, it's dying, Laura,
choked by its own useless shoots.
It's what happens when a living thing
is left to sprout untended.
What you have to do from time to time is cut it back,
trim away all that's sterile, unproductive.
Go all the way down to the root if need be.
Whatever it takes to make way for fresh growth.

Pause.

LAURA:
Why are we discussing gardening methods?

ROGER:
I'm like that rose.
It's what was happening to me.
I had to cut away all the unnecessary trappings
to bring out a better, healthier, more viable
version of myself.

LAURA:
You're not healthy, Roger. You're sick.

ROGER:
I'm only changing.
Change is a natural part of life.

LAURA:
Not for me.

ROGER:
Well that's the whole problem.

Silence.

ROGER:
Let's look at it this way.
For twenty-two years
you and I have been travelling together
down the same narrow road.
I admit that it's been smooth.
But now we've arrived at a junction.
I see a broad highway opening up,
leading into a magnificent new landscape.
Breathtaking vistas, as far as the eye can see.
I know this road is for me.
You can join me, Laura,
or else let me go, giving me your blessing.
But don't expect me to turn my back on it
just to keep you company.

LAURA:
It's a perilous road, Roger,
taking you off into the uncharted territory.
If I'm holding you back it's only for your own
protection.

ROGER:
You might as well try to hold back a waterfall.
Think of it, Laura:
the majestic beauty of a waterfall.
The force of those torrents cascading down a precipice,
the roar of them breaking into a million prisms
each with its own take on the world ...

See the mist rising above the fall,
the sun finding its way
through a soft, shimmering rainbow.
You can go and stand beneath the cataract ...
turn your face up ...
let the drops kiss your brow.
Cool water, clear as crystal,
pure as the light of day.
It's very refreshing, Laura.
Nothing to be afraid of.

LAURA:
(getting up) You're forgetting one thing, Roger.

ROGER:
What?

LAURA:
I don't like getting wet.

She leaves.

Ann Henning Jocelyn is a Swedish-born author, playwright and translator, based in Connemara since the early 1980s and working internationally. In Ireland she is perhaps best known for her much loved *Connemara Whirlwind* trilogy, already a classic, chosen to represent Ireland in UNESCO's International Youth Library. Her stage plays have been produced in countries as diverse as Ireland, Sweden and Bulgaria, and her dramatic translations of leading Scandinavian playwrights have received much acclaim. *Keylines*, a collection of her contributions to RTÉ's A Living Word has been published in several countries, and excerpts have appeared in a number of anthologies.

Joan McBreen

GROUND IVY
for Tom Mac Intyre

Athair lus, that name
you gave the ground ivy stays

Leaves cling,
twine, stubbornly hold.

The distance between us grows -
between earth, sky, stone, stream

as I try to draw close
to the nameless, the *doráithe*

at the heart of things.

LONDON IN DECEMBER

The air is cold between us,
a tuning fork for the words we use.

You shrug the collar of your borrowed coat.
We board a bus.
The misted window separates us
from passersby beyond
our touch, beyond our lives.

Snow turns to rain on the Thames.
I am cold to the bone,
to the very roots of my hair.

LOSS

Loss is a handkerchief on blackthorn touched with frost,
the imprint of your feet on sands you have crossed.

Loss is many stations where you waved in the rain,
the spring and summer you'll not see again.

Loss is the mother calling the boy who does not reply,
is forked lightning in a summer sky.

Loss is the last page of each book loved,
is in the bedroom curtains that have not moved.

Loss is the black gabardine never returned,
it has no colour - that too is learned.

Loss is a silence you cannot forget,
is tobacco smoke recalled in the lilac's garden where we
met.

SHADOWS

In winter from dark to light
I celebrate. Candles in cut glass
throw shadows over the room;
the souls of the dead know
what they know as they talk
into the night and still leave
imprints of their feet on the stairs.

Somewhere there is a man weeping
beside a woman he has beaten
and she is thinking about the time
before she allowed him to touch her in love,
when he took the picture of her on the bridge,
her elbows resting on stone,
a basket of windfalls at her feet
and her dress a water-colour blue.

Joan McBreen is from Sligo and lives in Tuam. Her poetry collections are *The Wind Beyond the Wall* (Story Line Press) and *A Walled Garden in Moylough* (Story Line Press and Salmon Publishing). Awarded an MA Degree from UCD in 1997, she compiled and edited *The White Page/An Bhileog Bhán: Twentieth Century Irish Women Poets* (Salmon Publishing 1999, 2000, 2001). Her latest collection, *Winter in The Eye: New and Selected Poems*, was published by Salmon in 2003. Her first CD, *The Long Light on the Land: Selected Poems by Joan McBreen with Traditional Airs and Classical Music*, was launched in 2004.

June Andrews

extract from HO HUM MOTEL

Wheat grass swayed in the August wind like waves on a yellow sea. A prairie dog uncoiled herself from her dozing pups and sniffed the air. In the long grass a young girl tugged at the dry wheat stalks and hollered into the twilight. One final push and the baby slid out, all bloody and grey and squirming. The long scissors she'd taken from her mother's sewing basket sliced into the umbilical cord. It reminded her of an oversized worm or the green water hose at the back of the house. Her auburn braids dangled down over the gewy mess. Pain skewered her insides and stole her breath. She curled up in the grass and fell into a sort of sleep.

A million stars invaded the inky sky; adding another secret to the centuries of little events gone unnoticed, in the shadowy world of man. And there it would stay, up there in the infinite sky; or in the minds of a few prairie dogs somewhere in the Alberta foothills.

In the distance a baby cried. Short gravelly bursts of sound pleading and demanding, pulling at the softness of her dreams; a maternal twisting and squeezing drove her to a part of herself she didn't understand. Sunday morning crept into the bedroom and surrounded her like a blanket. She'd unravel herself from her warm blankets and look around the room at the new curtains dotted with pink roses, the dolls in their usual spots on the dresser. She struggled back to the present and the bawls of baby-hunger grating at the vacant hills.

...

Dawn light reflected a dreamy incandescence off the stream of headlights moving along the Trans-Canada highway; radiant orbs gliding then disappearing over the horizon. She pressed the warm bundle to her chest and shivered inside the dirty sickness of her girlish body, now a heavy sac of blood and milk, piss and saliva. The lights from the filling station brightened with every queasy step, exposing her to an impervious world. The bathroom door squealed open on its rusty hinges then snapped shut. She slid her hand along the cold wall to find the light switch. The hard light exposed the tiny puckered face gazing out into an unfamiliar haze. And then she wailed, indignant, demanding, until an exploding breast plugged the gaping mouth, bitterly forcing the warm sweetness into her.

The Union 66 sign flashed fluorescent orange light onto the young girl, hurrying alone across the highway toward the river, then flickered out.

...

In late summer, trees dip their heavy branches into the cool water of the Bow River. The current pulls off the saturated leaves; they spin and drift then disappear under the dark water. Gordie Thomas tucked his good white shirt into his jeans. Normally he'd wear his suit for a special occasion, but he wanted to be comfortable. Birds whistled under a leafy canopy, fluttering from one tree to another along the meandering river. Gordie sat on the riverbank and answered back. The shrill vibrato echoed across the river.

Thin cloud-sheets dissolved in the misty heat of the morning. Soon the summer sun would scorch the arid town and hills surrounding it, a huge furnace blasting out of the clear blue sky destined to be another summer, like all the summers he could remember; nothing new. He lay down on the cool dirt resting his head on his hands.

Joe Kreske's rough country voice grizzled into the telephone.

'What's up with Gordie? He's not sick again, come on now, Minnie!'

Minnie fluttered around on the landing of their beer-bottle brown Duplex.

'Uh, well, no, not exactly Joe'.

'What the hell do you mean, not exactly?'

She paced back and forth, puffing on a cigarette.

'You know something Joe? I don't know where the hell he is, and I don't give a good God damned anymore! You tell that son-of-a-bitch to find himself another job and another wife!' Minnie slammed down the receiver then ran out of the house and down the street.

Gordie re-ran the last episode through his mind, safe under the soothing gusts of warmish wind.

'I can't do this anymore', Minnie said, with frustration and contempt.

'I'm sorry ... again'.

'You better call him. He's going to ask can you go this time! What the hell's wrong with you?' She raised her tone and tempo.

'Promise me this was the last time Gordie, promise me, or I'm going, we're going, me and Cal, back to Toronto'.

He shook his head, scattering the guilt from his mind and sat up rubbing his face. He opened up his bagged lunch and looked inside; pastrami on rye with mustard and two dill pickles, for desert a cream bun from Tommy Soo's bakery down town, and hot coffee with cream and sugar already mixed in his thermos.

Gordie chewed slowly; each bite of his sandwich relaying familiar satisfaction to his brain, removing him from the jaggedness of another day. And so it was, with his cream bun and coffee, until every crumb and every drop was gone. He looked at his watch. It was eleven-forty-five. He rubbed the sweat from his palms down the sides of his jeans and examined their etchings. New smaller lines had formed, shooting out randomly, crosses and flares cutting up through long tapered fingers.

He dropped his feet into the river. The cold water flooded indifferently into the top of his cowboy boots with a force that caught him off guard and made him afraid. He wanted to drag his feet back out and run. He'd change clothes and go into work, get a ribbing from the guys at the mill, maybe work on late to make it up, no big deal, he justified to himself. The current tugged off his boots and swallowed them into its watery gullet.

Minnie wandered back into his thoughts, her freckles and crab-apple cheeks, the spirals of ginger hair and the fire for life that burned inside her smallness. How the deception of marriage had created his boy Cal. His presence filled some remote corridor in their souls, rewarding them with a brief but absolute happiness. Still, he couldn't figure things out, get it right. Life was a series of muddled events seen through a frosty window, the people in his life skating aimlessly around him on a murky ice-rink. He'd miss nothing, he thought. Not the heat and colour of summer, nor the muffled silence of the first big snowfall at the end of autumn. Not even Cal.

Gordie slipped into the river and drifted along, bobbing and spinning with the current until the heaviness of his jeans and good white shirt quietly pulled him down.

Minnie searched through Gordie's desk looking for an 'I love you' or 'Sorry' but found nothing. She tried to remember the sound of his voice, the contours of his face under a perpetual nine o'clock shadow, or his slow lanky gait when he walked into the house, wary and searching. But she couldn't. He'd become a vague apparition; the by-product of a waking dream all gnarled up with expectation.

Cal Thomas tugged at the bottom of his favourite blue wool sweater with the shredded cuffs. It no longer covered the tubes of fat forming around his midriff. Minnie dabbed a fingerful of Brylcreem onto his thick rusty waves and brushed it through. Cal studied his freckly reflection in the long mirror stuck to the back of his bedroom door. Minnie's reflection smiled back with the same wild red hair, only hers was tamed into loose coils flipped up into a tube at the bottom, that always seemed on the verge of exploding free from Minnie's futile styling. He winced at their shared features.

'What are you scowling at? Elvis wasn't half as cute when he was ten!'

'Nothing. Why do we have to move?'

'A fresh start Cal ... I gotta get out of here'. Minnie tore off the cellophane and popped open the top of her Rothman's filter-tipped cigarettes. 'I can't take your daddy's family nosing around trying to blame me for what happened!'

'I don't want to move, I like it here!'

'Tough!'

Minnie left Cal alone in his bedroom to mope and connive with his reflection for a few minutes before they went to the funeral home to sort Gordie out.

Cal jammed Gordie's fishing rod into the casket, bending it up around the top of his head so it would fit in. The feathered hook jabbed the silky coffin liner, tearing a small hole in it.

'Jesus Christ! Do you have to put that thing in there?' Minnie winced and shut the door, blocking the view of the funeral director at the reception desk.

'He might want to fly-fish in heaven!'

The two stared numbly at Gordie's waxy face, his eyelids flat and shut, glued tight in death, sealing the empty sockets forever. The river had gnawed on his flesh, the shredded leftovers covered with gauze and the remains of his ravaged skin. His heavy leather brogues - conspicuous as the shoes on a shop window mannequin - flopped lifelessly to the sides of the coffin.

'Where's his boots?' Cal asked clacking Gordie's feet together then letting them flop over again.

'God knows. Stop touching him!'

Minnie finished fixing and straightening what seemed like a disinfected stuffed ghoul, then bent over the side of the coffin and kissed her husband passionately on his withered lips.

'Goodbye Gordie', she whispered.

'How can he be dead?' Cal kicked the side of the casket and cried. 'It's not fair! I want my dad, not this thing!'

'I'm sorry Cal'.

Rain fell like thick sweat from a rank oppressive sky onto Gordie's yellow cedar coffin. He was hoisted down to his final doss, in a small cemetery outside Calgary surrounded by his family and a dubious mixture of friends. After a pelting of reproachful glares and cheesy words of condolence, Minnie and Cal went home and packed.

...

Dust spiralled up from the road and settled on the car outside of the Union 66 filling station. Minnie flicked her cigarette butt through the open window, jumped out, and slammed the door. Cal got out and headed to the pop and candy machines by the gas station door.

'Fill 'er up!' Minnie said on her way to the bathroom.

Marcus John sauntered over to the car and lifted the spout, contemplating the tangle of ginger hair and slight warble of Minnie's bum, while the pungent gasoline poured into the side of the wood-panelled station wagon.

'Clean yer windshield?'

'Uh, yeah. Sure, that'd be swell', she answered, opening the bathroom door. Tiny feet pushed at the scratchy wool blanket until the dimpled skin touched the cold tiles.

'Jesus Christ!'

Minnie poked her head out of the bathroom. The Canadian Pacific Railway cars clunked noisily along the tracks to the west. She ran towards Marcus standing by the gas tank watching the train. The conductor pulled a cable and waved from his tiny window through the shrill blast of the train's horn. Marcus saluted as it passed. Minnie turned back, closing the dirty bathroom door behind her, then re-emerged with the bundle under her arm and hurried back to the car.

Cal plopped himself into the passenger seat and tore the wrapper off his jersey milk bar as they sped away from the gas station. Marcus John shook his head, watched the old station skid down the road toward Lyndon.

'What's the matter?' Cal asked.

'Nothing honey', Minnie answered, eyeing the rear-view mirror. 'I just want to get there'.

June Andrews is a Canadian writer, now living in Galway with her three sons. She worked as an Art Consultant in Vancouver, British Columbia before moving to Ireland in 1995. Her short fiction explores the inner lives of women from different indigenous tribes along the Pacific Northwest. She has completed a screenplay entitled *Black Lake* and is currently writing a novel, *Ho Hum Motel*.

Emily Cullen

BRADÁN FEASA DEARMADTA

Seanfhocal: *Éist le fuaim na habhann agus gheobhaidh tú breac.*

Tá bradáin ag streacailt
sa bhFeoir i gCill Chainnigh,
léimeann siad agus teipeann orthu.
Tá an bradán feasa ar sheachrán fada
chun teacht slán san Éire nua.
Tá ardmheas Finégas ar lár.
An bhfuil ár linn-ne ag dul amú
gan éisteacht leis na héisc?
Tá na coraí ró-ard
is gheobhaidh siad bás
muna n-éisteann muid arís
le síorfhuaim na habhann.

ARS MUSICA

If I were to score
the syncopation
of our relationship
there would be semi-quavers;
truncated harmonics;
plaintive semibrieves.
Reverberating silence -
a *glissando* of high drama,
some fluid viola moments
counterpointed
by an unruly xylophone
running away with itself.

Why this
when we showed the white feather
to five years of love?

Two Christmases later
I remove your red rib from its box
and learn to write anew.

I'm a troubadour writing at court:
about *joie* we forgot,
I try to soap ink off my hands -
must remember to blot.

Brazen, it lies across my desk:
a flyaway feather
from a flapper's cocktail dress
landed in some unlikely place.

The symbolism you ascribed
in a *frisson* of thought and flesh
we had a good chuckle then

Now it merely dips
then stretches across the page.

Is tú mo mhacasamhail:
mac mo shamhlaíochta,
macalla mo shamhailteacha.

A chomhthaistealaí,
cuireann tú ina luí
ar m'intinn
gur féidir mo scíth
a ligint
is beidh réiteach
ar gach scéal,
faoiseamh
ó chuile imní.

Cothaíonn muid
tearmann croí
ar scáth a chéile,
faoi anáil an duine eile,
is blathaím i ndídean
do ghlóir is do ghéaga,

ceann scríbe m'anama.

Emily Cullen comes from Co. Tipperary. She was the inaugural Arts Officer at NUI, Galway between 1999 and 2002. In 2004 she worked as Programme Director of the Patrick Kavanagh Centenary Celebrations. Emily's first poetry collection, *No Vague Utopia,* was published by Ainnir in 2003. She was selected by *Poetry Ireland* as an emerging writer for its Introductions Series. She is also a qualified teacher and performer of the Irish harp.

Jessie Lendennie

Excerpt from DAUGHTER

*She lay still and thought the sounds she heard were the
beginnings of comfort. Thought she could feel the sea on the
wind; the fall, falling of the waves. Wind sails riding the
horizon. The cold wash of the ocean against the walls of her
small room.*

...

Emma's mother straightened herself slowly, rubbing one
hand along her lower back. She stood and adjusted the
shoulder strap of the long canvas sack, half-full of
cotton, and turned to look at Emma who ran toward
her; then back to the row ahead. She squinted as the sun
caught her eyes. Heat shimmered across the field. She
lowered her head to tilt her wide-brimmed straw hat
against the glare.

...

*She lay still and the night moved past her. Branches brushed
the window. She wondered, as a child, of fingers tapping at
windows, of hands that reached out so softly to brush a cheek
... but never moved away.*
And the waves receded beyond the cliffs, beyond the trees.

...

Rows upon rows of cotton plants in the heat. Emma
watched the pickers moving along the rows, filling their
long trailing sacks. She rode the end of her mother's
cotton-sack, making patterns with her fingers in the

dust. She daydreamed lazily as the sack grew softer and her mother's pace slowed. She saw her sister running awkwardly behind them, heard her brothers arguing, and above her, her mother's mild voice.

...

In the darkness she imagined the silence at the centre of the wind. Hoped for the sound of rain; counted hours, years. Saw the morning path leading away between the cliffs.

EXILE SEQUENCE

1. Vision

and I wake again
at 4am
and from the back door
in a slip of light
I watch a black outline
against a neighbour's wall
marking the night
and later I dream
floating about the Florida islands
whose shining bridges
form one great Key
and the vision is a vast shape of water
coloured like neon cities
and the brightness,
which I had not remembered,
makes me, in my shape as air,
in my very being, a foreigner

2. America

Where were you going when you took up the stories
of all those lost people
and laughed across acres of fresh ploughed land
rolling, as a train through the desert
where were you going in that hot dust
your words burning the air
choking the breath of trees
Oh, I will always be here
where the smell of the wind become loss
and the turning of a simple leaf
the end of a lifetime.
And where you are now, how is it?
Do you still hear the tales from those who cannot
repeat your words, as I never could?
Am I silent as the sea, would I follow you
would I look beyond memories
because I have only these of you
strained toward the horizon,
covering the mountains
and I see you as I must see you,
sea and air, mountains and dust,
and the people who are your people
are not mine, not mine.

3. Displacement

Seventeen years, and you didn't go back,
not once
no, never
and not going back now
but backwards.
Is this a settling, as into old age
not longing, but boredom for my time
which was just too late?

Landscape?
Oh, yes, I miss the landscape
who would forget Great Salt Lake
or the Greyhound bus station at El Paso.
So many images, yes, and they haunt me
haunting as any puzzle or paradox
as any bus station at 2am
I didn't choose. The choice, however it was made,
came as thinly disguised as a sentence of an exile
when there is no native land.

Jessie Lendennie is a poet, and publisher with Salmon Publishing. She was born in Arkansas and moved to Galway in 1981. Widely anthologized, her collection *Daughter* was published by both Salmon Publishing and Signpost Press in the USA. Jessie was a co-founder of *The Salmon* magazine and the Cúirt International Festival of Literature in Galway. She currently lives near the Cliffs of Moher in Clare.

Kathleen O'Driscoll

BUTTERFLY

It was a lovely late September morning. She had thought of wearing a summer frock. But she felt very sophisticated at the moment, so she put on the skirt of her beige suit and a white blouse. She had great faith in the sun today. The white high-heeled shoes were pure summer, though it would be very hard to run in them. And there was so much to look at, it would be a miracle if she made the bus.

Looking straight ahead was hard, when on every side there were butterflies or strands of gossamer or birds or sunbeams reflected on flowers and windows and silvery lampposts. A leaf fell from one of O'Malley's trees. It felt a bit strange. It didn't fit in with the day. Oh Lord, if she didn't hurry, mass would be nearly over. It was a pity she had missed the quarter-to bus which came right up to Seamount. She would be a bit late. But, sure, what harm? She could pray very quickly.

The Augustinians felt dark after the white brightness of sky. Gradually the richer light from the stained glass showed the church to be quite full. She hopped into the back seat. There was a peace on week mornings that gave you time to think, that made God feel more ordinary than on Sundays. There seemed to be more old people too. The woman in front of her must have hurt her back because she didn't kneel down at all. Josephine inched a bit to the side on her knees, so she wouldn't be stuck up against her. She thought of her mother who had to work so hard with so many children to mind. And her father, a longshoreman, who was such fun on Sundays. He would bring all of them to a well, called The Watery, on the edge of Cork City and on the way he'd stop at the wild flowers that grew on walls and in footpath cracks and wasteland and give them little lessons that you wouldn't forget. Then he would sit them around the well and take a sweet for each one from a different pocket of his leather jacket. In the evening, around the fire in Blarney Street, he told stories of the ships and the sailors from far countries. And of the fairies, good and bad. And of people who were long dead or gone away to America.

Everyone stood up for the Gospel.

She hadn't thought of them much in a long time. The time was flying, indeed. If she got the earlier bus tomorrow she would go up to Our Lady's altar and light a candle for them.

It was dazzling white out in the street. She ran across and up the shade of Buttermilk Lane, took a quick look at Ryan's autumn fashions and on up to Lydon's. She just loved this part of the day. She returned the smiles of everyone in the bakery. She walked up the stairs to the café, slowing her step, gathering her dignity to face the ladies. They were all there before her, crowded around the little table. They had got out their summer frocks again and were rejoicing. They looked so gay. A beam of sunlight crossed them. The clamoured 'Good Mornings', making room for her. She ordered tea and eyed a white iced diamond on the large china plate in the middle of the table.

'We kept it for you', smiled Nancy in soft pink.

She touched the snow white starched tablecloth, lifted and tasted the little cake.

Chatting about the gorgeous day, she felt a small, shivery chill on her bare arms and one of them admired her tan against her white blouse.

They got to talking about the annual general meeting of Saint Joseph's Nursing Society. It had been yesterday and she was the new president. This made her feel proud.

'You looked very smart in her new hat, Josephine', Kathleen said, the moss green in her frock suiting her auburn hair. 'Did you get it specially?'

'Oh yes. Indeed I did. You know how Dr. Browne, the bishop, admires hats. And imagine, he said to me himself that I will make an elegant president'. She poured herself another cup of tea and one for Nancy.

Nancy said, 'It's a pity the clergy can't get married. Isn't it?'

But Josephine didn't think that at all. 'They wouldn't be half as interesting if they were married', she said, 'sure if they were going around doing the ordinary things married people do, they wouldn't appear very important'.

Anyway she loved her husband. In his birthday card last month she wrote, 'I love you more each year', and she meant that. But he just wasn't as interesting as a bishop. She wouldn't want him to be. Then lots of women might surround him and that wouldn't be so nice.

'Your hair looks marvelous in the sun', Bee said.

It was quite hard work keeping up with the roots. Rubbing like mad with cotton wool soaked in peroxide. But it was better to pretend it was no trouble at all. She was glad she had thought of going blonde. Looking at their wedding photograph, she seemed a bit serious with her dark hair. But very smart. And she remembered with pride her soft wool navy blue coat faced with powder blue and her velvet-soft navy suede shoes. And that little navy pleated frock underneath with its cream lace collar, so correct for a bride. She had bought an exquisite lace wedding frock and long tulle veil in Bournemouth beforehand. But the war interfered with their grand plans. Getting married from her sister's house in Dublin in the local church of Saint Teresa, Mount Merrion, was probably less frightening than a big ceremony in Cork, with everyone they both knew and all the relations. And his mother who was so beautiful and strong. And his father who was so silent and sad.

In Lydon's in the mornings after mass, there was no sadness. Today the tea and the cakes and the sun were perfect. And the friends. In no time at all they had to scatter for home. The pretty black haired cashier asked for her husband. That pleased her. Most of them lived around the Crescent and the leafy roads raying out from it, Nile Lodge, Taylor's Hill, Saint Mary's Road, Sea Road. She was the only one getting the bus today. She stood a few minutes at Brennan's stop. Brennan's window was a bit sensible and dreary today, all greys and browns. She thought she'd risk flying up to Moon's for a minute. She had an idea for an autumn suit and wanted to see what new materials Vinny had in, before talking to Mrs. Dunne about the style. Vinny was in charge of his department. He had wonderful taste. She thought of him as an old friend. She told him she'd like blue wool and he produced bale after bale of blues. Soft powder-blues to clear sky-blues to proud-Prussian blue to trim navy. But in a high corner she spotted the shade she wanted and he hauled it down with the help of the steps and spread it on the gleaming wooden counter for her. Oh, this was truly blue. Midnight-blue velvet. She had been planning an autumn suit, warm enough for the wind on more ordinary autumn days after this Indian summer time. But this blue velvet was too beautiful to leave until winter and it would make a lovely coat for mass on Christmas morning and the parties afterwards.

'Do you know Vinny, I think I'll take a snip of this for my Christmas coat. And maybe the sky blue serge for the autumn suit'.

He smiled quietly and cut the snippets for her to show to the dressmaker. She worried a little about when the bills would come and having to tell her husband.

Combien? he would ask or *Cé mhéad?* And then, 'You know, you're very extravagant. I can't really afford all that'.

'Old meanie', she would reply. Sometimes, when he was like that, she could kill him. But then he would be so proud of her being admired by everyone on the Christmas party round. And she might even get Mrs. Fortune to make a little velvet hat.

Running back down towards Brennan's stop she thought, 'Sometimes I'm sick of running'. And the bus flew past her.

'Oh God, I'll miss it', she cried out loud and her heart pounding. But it stopped and waited for her, though the stop was empty. The conductor said, 'Sure we'd have to wait for you, wouldn't we Ma'am'.

And she smiled thank you and searched her crowded white handbag for her purse.

'Bags are never big enough. Oh the relief of sitting down. There you are Peter. I was afraid I'd never find it', offering him a handful of bright coppers.

The town looked gay in the sun, now that she had time to watch it, like the ladies in their summer frocks. The trees along the Crescent were the smallest bit faded but there were still bright flowers peeping through gates and over walls. The gorgeous blue of delphiniums. And a delicious pure white blossom on her favourite rose bush in the world sticking out through a railing. She wished she could stop to bend to its perfume.

Salthill had the lovely, lazy, quiet feel of summer being over and all the visitors gone. She should really get out here and buy tomorrow's meat in Hallinan's. But it was nearly half one now. She would send her younger sister, Peggie, down on the bike after dinner. They would have a big argument about money and time and not be talking for a while. But then something nice would happen again. Peg would go to the dance in the Hangar and come home full of stories for the morning. Or her husband would sing 'I'll Walk Beside You' for her. Or one of the children would make her a daisy chain if there were enough daisies left.

The bus raced up the Prom like a horse to the winning post. She alighted not too carefully, in her white, high, high-heels and waved goodbye to the conductor and the driver and they turned back towards town.

She was sick and tired of the white high-heels by now. She would sit for a minute before heading up to the house. On the seat at the end of the road she laid her handbag beside her. The string-bag was still curled up inside. She realized she had no shopping at all. What harm though. The day was too good to be thinking of shopping. She looked up over the stony beach. Goodness, it was lovely. The Clare Hills were misty, with a line of light drawn under them. The sun was shimmering on the water. Its path was nearly silver. If only the world was like this every day. A red admiral butterfly lit on her shoulder. He seemed to be admiring a tiny pearl button on her blouse. And there was no one else at all to be seen. Everyone else in Galway must be sitting down to their dinner.

She loved them all in the house. But it was too nice and warm to be inside. And she was late and they would all get up and leave her at the table with the dirty ware and no one to talk to. She thought to herself, 'It's too nice to eat. Or wouldn't it be great if someone brought my dinner down here to me'. It was supposed to be called lunch now. But she felt like a little girl again. She didn't even want to be sophisticated, or only a bit.

The cold, clear winter they came here there were swans out there on the bay. She thought about the legend of the Children of Lir, who were transformed into swans for three hundred years. She would have to remember to tell it to her own brood tonight.

Kathleen O'Driscoll was born in Cork, lived around Ireland and Europe and now lives in Galway. *Goodbye Joe*, a poetry collection, and *Ether*, a short story collection, were both published by Caledon Press. Her poems have appeared in *Pillars of the House* (Wolfhound Press) and *The White Page* (Salmon Poetry). Her poems and stories have been published in many magazines and have been broadcast on local radio and RTÉ. She wrote and directed the short film, *Berlin Blues*.

Margaretta D'Arcy

SPITE AND ANGST IN LONDON, 1977

(i)

A chubby little man
a cosy couple
arm in arm
step in step
as they promenade the air:
squeeze the goolies
pull the hair
pick the kidneys.
The face crumples.
The eyes behind
(four eyes)
plead and become
a four-year old.
Why?
What have I done?
Why?
Because you are my Valentine.

You are my chubby
little teddy bear:
the swelling of the waist,
the hair like shortened waves
on its shelf,
the eyes still bright and merry
like an innocent soul.
Luck is mine
that you are
my Valentine.

...

To live in the conqueror's land
Is to be filled with Hate,
No comment without the barb
As I look at my enemy.
I wonder how they can walk with
Such confidence
With me watching them.
I snarl, they smile
And send invitations to my husband,
Nation shall speak peace to Nation:
What cheek.
Soft hand over mine
When I speak softly
But my fanatic gleam causes the hand
To withdraw
And caress the glass instead.

...

(iii)

Why should the sight of a determined
young woman
compelling hefty men in the street
to push her car through the snow
leave such lingering resentment in
my being?
The snub nose, short hair, young mouth and straight
blue eyes,
mouth set, on her errand up the
Broadway,
disturb me.
The dog is the giveaway.
Husband made a hole in their fence
at the bottom of their garden.
Freedom for the dog and freedom

for them.
But not for me, bloody nuisance. Destruction
for my garden.
Three or four times a day
I unlatch my back door
and thread my way through garbage
to observe my plants or
take a glance at the fence.
Telltale signs of black turds
going greyish in the rain
on my beds.
That damned dog with the intelligence
of its computer-programmed master
has knocked aside a loose board
in MY fence.
Why should I resent the wife most of all?
Because she's minding her own business
in front of my front window
and I'm not minding mine?

...

(iv)

To sneak in
to another's mind,
nestle and burrow,
stay quiet
and be the other:
sneak out
and going out
know
I have savoured for myself
you.

I would burrow
and sleep on the
waves of pain

and gently float
on the rhythms
within the other.

But the other
is not I.

And I still remain
me, having stolen
and squandered
what I could have had
if I remained outside.

Of course I know
I observe the other;
knowing is not the same
as offering myself
to be drained
Drained

                         ...

                        (v)

I sit and stare into space
Empty space of my house,
Neglected dust
Lies familiarly on the floor,
The table crowded out with papers.
But when I take up my pen
The room fills up
With scattered thoughts
Creating chaos where
Before there was orderly neglect.

...

The pain seeps as through a filter
into the sponges of hope
Even though the bands were to be removed,
it is not the bands holding it together
The inner one curled tight
not chewing his thumb
because he is unaware
the placenta has shrunk

Dried skin and bones
like a shaven rat
Only the teeth yellowish
grin through the
wizened face

(DATE UNKNOWN) BELFAST

I look out and see a ghost
walking down the road
the Falls Road
wet.
No taxis are about
to get it off the road
so It continues down.

Margaretta D'Arcy, originally from Dublin, has lived in Galway for many years. She is the founder of Radio Pirate-Woman, and co-author of many scripts for stage, TV and radio, including *The Non-Stop Connolly Show*, *Vandaleur's Folly* and *Whose Is The Kingdom?*, collaborations with John Arden. She is a member of Aosdána. Her book of memoirs, *Loose Theatre*, is coming out in the early summer of 2005.

Colleen Burns

Excerpt from ELEGY FOR GRACE

I hate to pack. Sudden notice, no thought beforehand. *Pascal's Letters to the Provincials*, *Rilke's Journals*, black calligraphy pens, rolls of rice paper, a fistful of paper clips shaped like dragonflies. Ten linen handkerchiefs. I count them out remembering my mother complaining that I was the kind who'd cry over a laundry list. Aspirin, toothbrush, shampoo. From the kitchen, tea-bags, black licorice vines to chew on the plane, from the night stand, Bertrand Russell's *Why I Am Not A Christian*. Running shoes, socks, sweat pants, sandals, T-shirt, tank top. I somehow manage to get it all in my overnight case. I'll wear my linen slacks, flax jacket, and floppy hat and sandals.

On the flight I am reading, trying to prepare myself for what will come when I arrive in Phoenix. I know her. I'll be ambushed and blindsided by her, by my misbegotten mother. The plane is on time but the car rental desk has lost my last minute reservation. They'll deliver it to her house by 4:00pm. It is 2:10 pm. Sunday.

Once the taxi pulls up to her curb, I step out to stare at the overgrowth. Red oleanders now cover the front windows facing the street. I can no longer see what was once my bedroom window. The Chilean mesquite's branches are so low they almost block the entrance to her driveway. What's it been - five years? I bend my head down to avoid tangling my hair in its thorns as I walk to her front door.

'It's about time'. My mother greets me as if I'd just stepped out to the nearest newsstand. She has no need for amenities such as, 'Hello, how are you? It's been a few years'. She's added a screen door with a double lock that she is swearing at as she turns the key. The contrast from the sun's glare to the darkness inside leaves me fumbling over the furniture.

I turn down her offer of a cup of coffee that I know will have been on the stove since breakfast. Some things you can count on. Once my eyes get used to the dark, I survey the living room for any additions or changes. The votive candles and the statues of St. Anne, the Virgin Mary, Jesus, Joseph, and Beethoven are in their assigned spots surrounded by the same vases of faded and dust-coated silk or paper flowers.

'Notice anything new?' she asks.

'No, but then I've only looked in the living room'.

'Check out the hallway', she prompts, as she stays in the kitchen drinking her coffee.

Above the credenza in a long horizontal line are framed photos, some cut from newspapers; all are hanging in identical black frames. I survey them in order of their appearance: Pope Pius XII, Joe Louis, Franklin D. Roosevelt, Vaughn Monroe, Mussolini, Edward R. Morrow, Jimmy Hoffa, Fulton J. Sheen, Fidel Castro, JFK, James Wong (her grocer).

'Vaughn Monroe?' is all I say.

'He can soak his socks in my coffee any day'.

Some things never change. 'I take it you aren't packed'.

'I will be as soon as you get that old Hartman suitcase from the top closet shelf. Pack the Christian Dior nightgown your father gave me the Christmas we left Minneapolis. It's wrapped in its original tissue in the bottom drawer and I want those rabbit-eared slippers your aunt gave me. They might look goofy but they sure as hell keep my feet warm'.

'It's ninety-two outside'.

'Pack the Lourdes water and don't give me that look. It's in the Guerlain perfume bottle with the purple stopper. And soap. I don't want that damn antibacterial stuff'.

'Is that it?' I ask, knowing how she loves giving orders.

'Pack those cold cream bars I got from Paris. Put in my wedding picture and that one of you standing next to the snowman. Be sure to dust them first. Should I take my pearls? Put them in just in case'. She raises her voice to tell me, 'Take my crossword puzzles and this month's *Reader's Digest* on the night stand. That should be it. Oh, put my monogrammed silk pillowcase in too. I hate those muslin excuses for sheets. Can you think of anything else?'

'Your radio? Rosary?'

'Hell, yes. I forgot. Oh, and take down my big wall clock and bring it along. I want you to hang it straight across from my bed so it's the first thing I see when I look up. I happen to like to keep track of time, unlike you and those hippies you hang around with'.

'Yes. The Bank of America is packed with hippies. Wall to wall'.

'How'd you get off work?'

'I told them I was taking vacation for three days'.

'Aren't you the optimist? Oh, run back and get my denture brush, for God's sake'.

She's announced that we're going to Lulu Belle's in Scottsdale before she checks in to the hospital.

My mother orders black raspberry crepes with ice cream and whipped cream, telling the waiter, 'I might as well be hung for a sheep as a lamb'. She lowers her voice as she turns to tell me, 'This could be my last meal'.

'I hardly think so, mother'.

'Call me Grace. You look too old to be my daughter. I'd order raspberries every time. Just in case'.

'I have yet to get a straight answer from you'.

'I've already told you. They want one of my lungs. By the way, this doctor looks like he comes to work on a skateboard, so when you meet him, don't make jokes about his age. He doesn't appreciate the fact he looks fourteen, but then, neither do I'.

'What is it? Which one?'

'Cancer. Left'. She hands me a large brown envelope that includes the doctor's letter and the hospital registration forms. I sift through a sheaf of papers. It is clear that my mother has lung cancer. I hide my horror by asking 'Why did you wait until now to tell me?'

'I didn't want to worry you'.

Oh, sure. While I'm still trying to buy time to absorb all of this, I manage to ask, 'How long did you smoke?'

'Never inhaled'.

'That's not what I asked'.

'Doesn't matter. I quit the day he told me. I've been smoke-free for six days and seven hours. Listen, I've started my will. I'll dictate it to you after we check in'.

Between bites, she's started to outline what she wants to leave to each of her sisters. She tells me that she is skipping the families of the ones who are dead.

I order more coffee.

'The main thing is I want the sterling to go to Lily. I bought all ten place settings in an estate sale. I never told you they belonged to F. Scott Fitzgerald. The dents in those spoons are worth a fortune. Zelda threw them at Scotty whenever they got drunk and fought during dinner, which was most of the time the way I heard it. Between that and their dogs, they got broken in. Lily will appreciate them. She's always been the literary one. Speaking of literary, I want you to write my eulogy'.

'We don't need to worry about that now'.

'Yes, we do. I want to hear it and be sure it covers everything'.

As we leave the parking lot of the restaurant, Grace spots a North Dakota license plate.

Still trying to get a handle on this, I ask, 'Who's had cancer in our family?'

'Depends on who you ask'.

'This isn't Twenty Questions, damn it'.

'There's more on your father's side than mine'.

'We're talking about you. Your lung. Your odds'.

'Who needs odds? I've said a novena to St. Jude'.

'What did Grandma die of?'

'Your father's mother was the most ill-timed woman I ever met. Died on Thanksgiving - for spite. A stroke, I think'.

Not in the mood for her games, I stay silent.

'OK. Ask me anything. I've always been the memory for my whole family. Cancer. Cancer. Old age. Heart attack. Old age. In that order. How much did you leave for a tip?'

It's as I knew it would be. You'd think a five-year absence would help. You'd think that it would take more than a few hours before I'd be getting a migraine and looking for exits. There's a lot to be said for not being an only child. If I had a sister or two, we could spend time arguing over whose turn it was to deal with her. Even brothers, though they'd never know what to do. Once Grace is checked in and in her room, I get a chance to talk to her physician. He thinks it's a straightforward case. He doesn't know Grace. I guess he means they'll have caught it in time so she can expect a full recovery. I wonder if that'll disappoint her. Much as she loves being alive, she loves upstaging everyone more. Tonight, I'm going to stay at the house. I know that after the surgery, she won't let me out of her sight. She's already arranged for a cot to be put in her room so I can 'live' with her.

I called Mae tonight to tell her that it looks like I won't make it back for two, maybe three, weeks. I know Mr. Casey won't mind. He calls me his best bank-teller but only because I have a college degree and perfect attendance neither of which make much difference. Poor man. He's the world's nicest guy who must've had dreams but married too young and got locked in with a brood of little Irish Catholics. God save me from such a fate. This house smells just as it did when I left, when I packed and ran, the day after university commencement which I paid $40 to get out of. Mae and I drove nearly nonstop in her rattle-trap of a car that miraculously made it to Barstow before it died. Between us, we had just enough cash to take the bus to the city, leaving most of our stuff including car-parts in a storage shed at an industrial park. San Francisco - Mae's city of origin, my city of choice. What was it I ran from?

My freedom has not been all it was cracked up to be, has not been as complete as the dictionary promised. Sometimes I think I'm living under its second or third definition.

Cigarette smoke, stale linens, layers of rancid perfumes - my old bedroom smells like the rest of the house now. The dust is thicker than pollen on the bookshelves above the bed with its framed photos, the foreign looks on my face: me at four, at my first piano recital, wearing a lace dress and blackened Band-Aids on my scabby knees, socks that don't match, and that perpetual frown. I'm seven in my First Communion photo and in this one I wear a look of pained bewilderment, my head tilted to the left like our dog's, white dress and veil, with my mother furious about my sagging long stockings. She kept telling me to pull them up. They were up.

This next one is a glossy eight by ten of me as a grinning Catholic Breck girl: pious, smarmy, tight-assed obedient. I'm wearing a pleated navy blue skirt, white

Ship and Shore blouse, Sacred Heart Badge and Sodality pin. All I wanted was to be a saint, but not just any kind of a saint. I must die a virgin martyr.

In the top drawer of what was once my dresser, there's my St. Andrew Daily Missal still gilt-edged and jammed with holy cards; its grosgrain ribbons marking invocations, convocations, prayers for vocations. In the next drawer I rummage through an old Whitman's candy box full of snapshots; photos of my friend, Barbara and me in our hiding place in the swamp on the edge of her farm. That was the year we suddenly moved to the country. I took the school bus for the first time. Barbara was the only one who'd sit with me because I was a 'city slicker'.

Here's a picture of Andrea, the blind girl, and me. I was assigned to be her guide at Girl Scouts' Summer Camp. We still lived in the city of Minneapolis then, where we had a real house with a garden and a fenced-in green lawn. I owned white ice-skates and had a sandbox.

I gather up a few pictures of Grace knowing the ones that'll matter to her and I throw in a few of the two of us when I was a baby. Maybe she'll talk, tell me about us for a change, or before I was born, before she married, any thing but the damn Donnelly clan. I'm due back at 7:00 am. Tonight, I'll sleep on the back porch, make myself a pillow from folded bath towels. This old porch is all too familiar but without the house's unsettling odors.

Cancer. Stupidly, I've never thought of her as mortal. Not Grace. Tonight, though, I am mostly just furious with her, for ambushing me. This is so like her - doing her hat tricks, pulling out trump cards, springing her news, relishing the shock she can still generate.

Where the hell is an alarm clock?

Colleen Burns is an Irish-American who lives in Arizona and in Oughterard. She worked in academia before retirement.

Sharon Murphy

Two songs

GREAT DARK ONE

Great dark one,
Did your dreams die
When they came to steal your mind?
They want mine. Why?

Chorus:

If I could speak my heart,
If I could lie with you,
I would wail so loud
While you held me in your ancient arms.

Great dark one,
When I looked at you
I saw you without beauty
Because I learned to look with their eyes
And learned to believe their lies.

Chorus:

If I could speak my heart,
If I could lie with you,
I would wail so loud
While you held me in your ancient arms.

The masters of supremacy
Have pulled us apart in their greed,
But the river flows with our tears,
She's flowing four hundred years,
But the river flows with our tears;
She's flowing. She's growing four hundred years,
She's flowing. She's growing with our tears.

MAMA

I am just a kid,
I've walked through Hell's doors,
Mama, why leave me there, alone?

They tell me they're my masters now,
'Do what we say!'
You gave them that power,
And I must obey.

My home is St. Joseph's school,
Lots of kids around.
What happened, Mama,
Did you try, or just walk out?

It's not easy, Mama,
To be lost in the crowd.
They say I must be grateful,
I got food in my mouth.

Where are you, Mama?
Was it hard to go your way?
Do you still remember me?
Or have I faded away?

Singer/songwriter **Sharon Murphy** grew up in Connemara
and now lives in Galway city. Many of her songs deal with
personal and social issues, and her début CD, *Invisible Walls*,
containing thirteen original songs, is on release in Ireland.

Muireann Ní Bhrolcháin

Ó DIALANN CHAOIMHE

Líon Aoife babhla ildathach le calóga arbhair agus chuir an citeal ar siúl. Thosaigh sé ag geonaíl; ní raibh dóthain uisce ann. Chaith sí muga eile isteach ann agus stán amach ar an ngairdín cúil. Bhog a croí ar fheiceáil solas na gréine di, agus an spéir ghorm gan scamall. Arbh fhéidir go raibh biseach ag teacht ar an aimsir, an samhradh ag teacht i gceart? D'fhéadfaidís dul síos ar an trá tar éis na scoile!

Chuir sí mála tae isteach sa mhuga ildathach a bhí ar aonphatrún bláthach leis an mbabhla. Thaitin lena máthair go mbeadh gach aon ní sa teach ag teacht le chéile agus d'éirigh léi le deireanas cur gréithe cistine a aimsiú a bhí ar aon dul leis an bpáipéar balla. Bhíodh Aoife agus a hathair ag magadh fúithi, ach thaitin le hAoife féin féachaint ar na gréithe ildathacha uile ar an mbord, áit ar leag a máthair iad an oíche roimh ré. Bhíodh a cairde de shíor ag moladh a máthar, rud ar éirigh Aoife bréan de. Dar léi nárbh aon chúis mholta í a máthair. Shuigh sí ag an mbord ag baint taitnimh as an gciúnas gan fiú an raidió a chur ar siúl.

... B'fhéidir go bhfeicfeadh sí féin agus Aisling é ar a mbealach chun na scoile. An rothar rásaíochta corcra agus bán, a chuid gruaige ag séideadh sa ghaoth. Tomás. Chorraigh a croí ag smaoineamh air. Ba bheag seans a bhí aici labhairt leis cé nach raibh sé ina chónaí' ach cúpla céad slat siar an bóthar uaithi féin. Ach bhí sé go hálainn - díreach cosúil le Christian Slater. Ní raibh sé ar aon scoil léi - níor shíl a máthair gur mhaith an rud é Aoife a bheith ar scoil mheasctha, agus cuireadh chuig scoil cailíní í. Ní hamháin sin, ach scoil de chuid na mban rialta! D'fhreastail Tomás ar scoil buachaillí díreach in aice lena scoil féin. Bhí an dá fhoirgneamh buailte ar a chéile agus na háiseanna céanna spóirt acu ... ach níor leor é sin d'Aoife. Theastaigh uaithi aithne níos fearr a chur ar Thomás. Conas a d'fhéadfadh sí sin a dhéanamh agus iad scartha óna chéile agus gan cead amach aicise?

'Ceapann siad go bhfuilimid fós deich mbliana d'aois! Ní thuigeann siad dada! Is dóigh leo go bhfuilimid ag maireachtáil sa mheánaois ar fad!' a deireadh Aoife lena máthair agus iad ag argóint faoin scoil. 'Agus mar an gcéanna libhse - is féidir le gach duine eile dul chuig an dioscó ach amháin mise'.

'Éist anois, a Aoife, níl ann ach bliain amháin eile go dtí scrúdú an Teastais Shinsearaigh', a dúirt a máthair léi an uair dheireanach dóibh ag argóint. 'Tig leat do rogha rud a dhéanamh nuair a fhágfaidh tú an scoil - ach go dtí sin déanfaidh tú mar a deirimse leat. An dtuigeann tú é sin?'

Lean sí uirthi gan fanacht le freagra.

'Tuigimse go maith gur mhaith leat a bheith ag freastal ar scoil mheasctha, ach tá a fhios ag an domhan go n-éiríonn níos fearr le cailíní ...'

Chríochnaigh Aoife an abairt di: '... i scoileanna nach bhfuil measctha!'

...

Maidin Dé hAoine a bhí an argóint dheireanach acu. Seachtain iomlán agus is ar éigean gur labhair Aoife lena tuismitheoirí ó shin. D'oscail sí an cuisneoir agus thóg amach píosa den sicín a bhí fágtha ann. Thosaigh sí ag déanamh a cuid ceapairí go mall. Ba bheag nár ghearr sí a méar agus í ag smaoineamh agus ag pleanáil conas a d'fhéadfadh sí teacht ar dheis labhartha le Tomás. B'fhéidir go raibh fuascailt na faidhbe aici ... bhuel, ag Aisling. Ise a smaoinigh ar an tseift. Bhí Tomás páirteach sa Chumann Drámaíochta sa bhaile mór, cumann a léirigh drámaí Gaeilge i rith na bliana. Cé gur amaitéaraigh iad na haisteoirí, tugadh cúpla punt dóibh as ucht gach dráma agus theastaigh ó Aoife a bheith páirteach ann freisin. Bhí sí chun iarraidh ar a tuismitheoirí anocht. Bhuel, chuirfeadh sí ceist ar a hathair i dtosach agus ansin ar a máthair. B'fhéidir go mbeadh seisean níos tuisceanaí. Thaitin drámaí leo beirt. B'fhéidir go bhfeicfidís fiúntas sa smaoineamh. Ní dioscó a bheadh ann.

...

'Bhuel ... inis dom! Cén chaoi a raibh sé? Cé a bhí ann?'

Gháir Aisling faoina cara.

'Cad a tharla? Caithfidh tú insint dom!'

'Fuist!' arsa Aisling. 'Cloisfidh an tSiúr Máire thú!'

'Ar aghaidh leat mar sin! Inis dom. Cad a tharla?'

'Bhí Tomás ann - sin a theastaigh uait a chloisteáil, nach ea? Ná séan é! Féach ort ag deargadh san aghaidh!'

'Nílim ag deargadh san aghaidh!' arsa Aoife go borb léi. 'Inis dom fút féin ... agus gach éinne eile. Cé a thug abhaile tú?'

'Ní ligfinn do na leaideanna sin mé a thionlacan abhaile! Páistí atá iontu uile. Tháinig mé abhaile le Máire agus Siobhán ... ach ...'

Stop sí.

'Ar aghaidh leat! Inis!'

'Bhí Tomás, Caoimhín agus Breandán linn freisin'.

Ní raibh bac ar bith ar Aisling dul chuig damhsa nó dioscó. Thug a máthair cead di freastal orthu uile agus bhí Aoife go mór in éad léi.

'Shiúil Tomás abhaile libh? Cé leis ...?'

Ní fhéadfadh sí an abairt a chríochnú. Bhí a croí i mbonn a cos. Bhí sé caillte aici mar nach raibh cead aici dul chuig an dioscó. Ní labhródh sí lena máthair go deo arís!

...

Nuair a d'fhill Aoife ón scoil tar éis an chluiche chispheile, bhí carr a máthar taobh amuigh den teach.

'Hóra! A Mham? Cá bhfuil tú?'

Is ansin a chuala sí monabhar éadrom an raidió. Ní raibh a máthair in ann í a chloisteáil. Chuaigh sí suas an staighre, dhá chéim in éineacht. Bhí doras sheomra a tuismitheoirí dúnta.

Bhí na cuirtíní bándearga tarraingthe agus an raidió ag dordán. Bhí a máthair sínte siar ar an gcuilt agus a súile dúnta. Shiúil sí isteach sa seomra i dtreo na leapa a bhí taobh thiar den doras. Chorraigh a máthair beagán ach níor dhúisigh. Shiúil Aoife níos gaire di ar na barraicíní ar fhaitíos í a mhúscailt. Bhí rian na ndeor le sonrú ar a haghaidh - cad a bhí cearr? Cad a thabharfadh ar a máthair gol? Is ansin a chonaic sí an leabhar ina haice, leabhar ait agus clúdach de pháipéar donn air, pictiúir agus scríbhneoireacht ann. Chrom sí go cúramach agus d'fhéach ar an gceannteideal air.

CÍN LAE CHAOIMHE
DIALANN 1970

Dialann a bhí ann! Dialann lena máthair nuair a bhí sí - rinne sí an suimiú go tapa - seacht mbliana déag. An aois chéanna ina raibh sí féin anois! An dialann a thug uirthi gol. Cad a d'fhéadfadh cur as chomh mór sin di tar éis na mblianta? Nár bhreá léi féin í a léamh, agus eolas a fháil ar cad a bhí ag titim amach i saol a máthar nuair a bhí sí ar comhaois léi féin - na smaointe a bhí aici, agus an eachtra mhistéireach a bhain caoineadh as a máthair go háirithe.

Sracfhéachaint eile ina treo. Í fós ina codladh. Tharraing sí chuici an dialann. D'fhéach sí ar an leathanach a bhí á léamh ag a máthair sular thit a codladh uirthi. Tús na dialainne - Eanáir. Thosaigh sí ar an leathanach a iompú ach chorraigh a máthair. Go mear, chuir sí an dialann ar ais ar an leaba, díreach mar a fuair sí í. D'éirigh a máthair ina suí agus chuimil a súile.

'Aoife? Cén t-am é? An bhfuil tú i bhfad anseo? Thit mé i mo chodladh'.

Thug Aoife faoi deara í ag caitheamh súilfhéachana ar an leabhar, ag cinntiú go raibh sé fós ann. Gan focal a rá thóg sí é agus chuir sa tarraiceán ina haice go tapa. D'fhéach sí ar Aoife.

'Níl mé ach díreach tagtha isteach', arsa Aoife. 'Tá brón orm má dhúisigh mé tú. Ní raibh a fhios agam cá raibh tú. B'fhéidir gur mhaith leat cupán tae?'

Bhí dearmadta aici gur thug sí geall gan labhairt lena máthair.

'Bheadh sé sin go haoibhinn', a d'fhreagair sí. 'Mar a fheiceann tú, bhí mé ag iarraidh an vardrús sin thall a ghlanadh amach'.

D'oscail Aoife a béal agus í ar tí labhairt, ach chuimhnigh sí ansin nach raibh sí in ainm is a bheith ag labhairt léi - cé go mbeadh uirthi rud éigin a rá tráthnóna nuair a chuirfeadh sí ceist uirthi faoin amharclann. D'éirigh sí den leaba agus thug aghaidh ar an staighre chun an tae a dhéanamh. B'fhearr di iarracht éigin a dhéanamh a bheith deas léi.

...

'Fág an muga ar an mbord ansin', ar sí, beagán níos boirbe ná ba ghnáth. Mhaolaigh sí an tonn ansin, áfach. 'Maith an cailín, go raibh maith agat. Anois, ar mhiste leat rud éigin eile a dhéanamh? An bhféadfá cipín a chur leis an tine sa seomra suí? Tá a fhios agam go bhfuil sé te anois ach éireoidh sé fuar níos deireanaí. Tosóidh mé féin ar an dinnéar. Beidh Tony sa bhaile luath anocht'.

Tony a hathair. Níor thug a mháthair riamh Daid air mar a thabharfadh tuismitheoirí eile.

Thug Aoife sracfhéachaint ar an urlár. Bhí leabhair scaipthe ar fud na háite - beag, mór, sean, nua - agus iad uile breac leis na focail chéanna:

CÍN LAE CHAOIMHE

Bhí an bhliain scríofa ina dhiaidh sin i ngach cás. Chuir siad an ceann eile i gcuimhne di - 1970 - ach ní raibh ceann na bliana sin le feiceáil aici go hoscailte. Is dócha go raibh sé fós sa tarraiceán in aice na leapa.

'Cad iad sin?' a d'iarr Aoife, ag iarraidh a glór a choimeád chomh neamhurchóideach agus ab fhéidir léi.

'Mo chuid dialann ... nach mé atá ag éirí sean! Is deacair creidiúint go bhfuil an oiread sin acu ann! Tá mo shaol uile ar an urlár!'

'An féidir liom féachaint orthu?' a d'iarr Aoife uirthi go tobann.

'Cad é?'

'Na dialanna ... an féidir liom féachaint orthu?' a dúirt sí arís.

'Agus cén fáth a dteastódh uait féachaint orthu siúd?' arsa a máthair. 'Níl faic iontu sin ach an saol atá thart. Is mór an spraoi domsa iad, ach ní thuigim cén tarraingt a bheadh agatsa orthu!'

'Cé mhéad acu atá ann?' a dúirt Aoife.

'Nílim cinnte. Ba chóir go mbeadh ceann agam do gach aon bhliain ón uair a bhí mé 13, fan soicind ... sin ...'

'1966', a d'fhreagair Aoife go tapa.

'Níl locht ar bith ar an matamaitic agat!' a dúirt a máthair agus meangadh gáire ar a béal.

Thóg a máthair an dialann ba ghaire di, 1971, agus an chéad cheann eile, 1972.

'Ní dóigh liom go bhfuil siad ar fad agam. Tá cuid acu in easnamh, caillte', a dúirt a máthair go scinnideach. Léim sí den chathaoir agus thosaigh ag bailiú na leabhar agus á leagan ar an leaba ceann ar cheann.

D'fhéach Aoife uirthi. Bhí rud éigin á cheilt aici. Cad a bhí sa leabhar a bhí sa tarraiceán? Cén mhistéir a bhí sna dialanna?

'Lig dom ceann amháin acu a léamh ar a laghad', a d'impigh Aoife uirthi. 'Ceann amháin, do rogha féin. Le do thoil?'

Thug a máthair sracfhéachaint uirthi agus thóg ceann de na dialanna ina lámh, scrúdaigh agus shín chuici í.

'Ceart go leor. Bíodh an ceann seo agat. Ach ná bí chugam ag lorg a thuilleadh'.

Thóg Aoife an dialann a tairgeadh di agus d'fhéach ar dháta an chlúdaigh - 1969. An bhliain díreach roimh bhliain na dialainne eile. B'fhéidir go mbeadh leid ann a thabharfadh eolas éigin di faoin gceann eile. Tháinig sceitimíní uirthi, í ar bís ag tnúth lena léamh. D'fhág sí an seomra sula mbeadh seans ag a máthair athchomhairle a dhéanamh, í ag suimiú go tapa ina ceann: Sé bliana déag a bhí a máthair i 1969, bliain níos óige ná mar a bhí sí féin anois. A leithéid! Go mbeadh seans aici a haigne a iniúchadh agus í ar comhaois léi féin. Bhí sí den tuairim gur chóir di féin dialann a choinneáil. Nárbh aoibhinn a bheith dá léamh sna blianta le teacht, ag smaoineamh siar ar na seanlaethanta ... ach stop sí. Cad a bheadh le scríobh aicise i ndialann? Cad a tharla di arbh fhiú a bheith ag coinneáil dialainne ina thaobh? Dada! Ní scaoilfeadh a máthair amach í;

níor tharla aon eachtra neamhghnách ina saol. Cúrsaí samhraidh sa Ghaeltacht - sin a raibh ann go dtí seo. Agus Tomás. Ach cad a d'fhéadfaí a scríobh faoi Thomás nuair nach raibh seans aici é a fheiceáil fiú - gan trácht ar chomhrá a dhéanamh leis! Bhraith sí arís an fhearg a líon a croí níos luaithe. Bhuel, b'fhéidir go mbeadh fuascailt na faidhbe sin aici anois - míniú ar mheon a máthar.

Shuigh sí chun boird ar feadh scaithimh ag stánadh ar an bpáipéar balla os a comhair amach, í ag smaoineamh ar Thomás. Ag brionglóideach go gcasfaí ar a chéile iad maidin éigin agus í ag dul chun na scoile agus go dtabharfadh sé cuireadh di dul chuig an dioscó ... nó chuig dráma san amharclann, agus go n-inseodh sé di sa dorchadas go raibh sé ag tnúth le casadh uirthi ... Ach cén mhaitheas di a bheith ag brionglóideach mar sin? Nach raibh a fhios aici go maith nach bhféadfadh sí dul chuig an dioscó nó chuig an dráma - fiú dá bhfaigheadh sí cuireadh. A máthair arís, agus a hathair nár thug tacaíocht ar bith di ina coinne ach a deireadh de shíor; 'Éist le do mháthair anois - tá ciall aici'.

Thóg sí a mála scoile agus lig osna throm. Bheadh uirthi bealach éalaithe a chinntiú trí na leabhair. Bhí an ceart ag a tuismitheoirí sa mhéid sin - an Ollscoil an seans éalaithe a bheadh aici. Níorbh fhiú freastal ar Ollscoil na Gaillimhe. Rachadh sí go Baile Átha Cliath, áit ina mbeadh saol dá cuid féin aici, saoirse agus neamhspleáchas.

Muireann Ní Bhrolcháin was educated at UCG and lectures in Medieval Irish Studies at NUI Maynooth. Her research on An Banshenchas is forthcoming from Four Courts Press. She is the author of 5 books from Clo Iar-Chonnachta, *Ar Ais Arís, An Solas sa Chaisleán, Dialann Chaoimhe, Eachtraí Samhraidh* and *An Bád sa Chuan* which won an Oireachtas prize.

Patricia Burke Brogan

PATTERNS

Rhythm of water
pleats and folds
on river mouth
at Labasheeda.

Pulse of jet-planes
from Moscow, from Boston
shudder above Ardnacrusha.

Rhythm of stone axe
on straight-grained poplar
shaped and carved this canoe.

Heartbeat of a child
swells from a womb-canoe
below Saint's Island.

In Kiladysert
the child plays
with mud-patterns
from the estuary.

With a blue crayon
she makes word-patterns,
finds a river poem.

The play takes place at Samhain, when boundaries between living and dead dissolve. SISTER LUKE, a former Superior of Killmacha Magdalen Laundry, returns to her convent, which is being demolished.
She writes her stories on her starched guimpes.
(Guimpe - A stiffly starched piece of white linen worn over the chest).
SISTER LUKE is dressed in veil-coif-domino-guimpe with black habit of pre-Vatican 2 nun's clothing.

Act 1 Scene 3

SISTER LUKE hangs her page-guimpes by their tapes on what remains of convent walls.

Sister Luke: Chapter 3. My life story? First I must -

(She hums, Ar maidin moch do gabhas amach -, as she writes, NO DUMPING on a guimpe, attaches it to a post set into rubble downstage right, returns to her chair-copter and sits down).

Now we're ready!

(She takes up another guimpe and continues to write).

When I was appointed Superior in Killmacha Magdalen Laundry, I changed the so-called penitents' diet. I insisted that they got plenty of milk and fresh vegetables. The finest potatoes, cabbages, onions and herbs grew in our convent garden and we had our own milch cows. I only had to remember my own time in the Novitiate, when the smell of rashers frying for His Lordship's breakfast made me cry with hunger, made me lonely for home.

I spent the Laundry money on the women instead of sending it on to Central Powers. I bought them tennis shoes, I took away their ugly boots. I gave them flowery aprons instead of clay-coloured overalls -

Come over and look into the crater under that red-toothed bull-dozer.

(She moves downstage to the 'crater').

Hundreds and hundreds and hundreds of worn-out boots, torn aprons, all holding their own pain! -

I led the women outside to landscape the grounds, to build and decorate my Lourdes Grotto. Mary and Bernadette amidst petunias, arabis and columbines. Our Magdalena and our Katie amidst lupins and Canterbury bells! To let fresh air instead of bleach-fumes into their lungs. Wasn't I right? Wouldn't Christ Himself do the same? Did I tell you that my sister and myself brought big dowries into the convent with us? Money helps everywhere. Even in a convent.

(She places another page-guimpe on stage floor as lights change).
Sound: Fast convent-bell sounds.

Another page for my book! Soon I'll have a tent of story-pages. Like Saint Paul. Saint Paul was a tent-maker. He escaped from his enemies in a basket. Our poor Rosemary tried to get away in a Laundry basket. She wanted to see her baby son in Saint Finbar's Orphanage. When that failed her, she tied bed-sheets together and lowered herself from the dormitory window. We found her next morning. Yes! - Sheets weakened from boiling in the big machines. Her poor neck broken! No, it wasn't suicide! No. That was poor Mary Ann. With a bottle of bleach! Rosemary and Mary Ann were buried over near that big chimney. Last week the builders exhumed and cremated them - and all the others. - That big chimney? No! No! It's not a crematorium chimney! It's the laundry chimney! Dust to dust. Into dust thou shalt return. - Mary Magdalene was wronged as well. The crowd, who wanted to get rid of her said she was a great sinner. And she the first witness of the Resurrection! We'd never have heard about Easter morning only for Mary Magdalene and those brave women. The other Apostles ran away! - Ordain women? - The Vatican forbids us to even discuss it! - Shhh! But, I must write the truth about those early Christian women. Luckily, I've eternity before me! -

(Sings)

> Ar maidin moch do gabhas amach ar bhruach
> Loch a Léin
> An Samradh teacht 'san chraobh le n'ais
> 'gus lonnra te ó'n ngréin
> Ar taisteal dhom tré bhailte poirt agus bánta míne ré -

(Lights low)

Act 1 Scene 4

Lights up. SISTER LUKE picks up another guimpe and pauses.

Sister Luke: Another Chapter! We have this new chaplain, Father James. Out of your mind good-looking! Gorgeous! Over six foot tall. Big grey-blue eyes that'd look through you, dark hair, skin not seminary-looking. A voice like a cello. No! More like a double bass. Such a change from nuns' voices.

(She stands, moves to right and chants in soprano tones).

In nomine Patris, et Filii, et Spiritus Sancti.

(FATHER JAMES, in alb, chasuble and stole, is seen behind stained glass window).

Father James: *(Chants)* In nomine Patris, et Filii, et Spiritus Sancti.

Sister Luke: *(Chants)* Amen!

Father James: *(Chants)* Introibo ad altare Dei.

Sister Luke: *(Chants)* Ad Deum qui laetificat juventutem meum.

Father James: *(Chants)* Judica me, Deus, et discerne causum meam de gente non sancta: ab homine iniquo et doloso erue me -

(Lights change. FATHER JAMES exits. SISTER LUKE moves downstage).

Sister Luke: Didn't put on an awwccent like His Lordship. I never took my eyes off you, when you were on the altar, Father James. Custody of the eyes, God forgive me! But, God did forgive me. I'll tell you how I know!

(Looks straight ahead).

Sister Benedict came to my cell when I was at death's door, just about to take off! I was screaming at the top of my voice.

(Screams)

I'm damned, I'm damned for all eternity! I'll go to Hell, because I kept looking at Father James instead of keeping custody of the eyes. -

(SISTER BENEDICT, wrapped in white sheets, her arms extended like wings, enters from the cloisters and stands upstage between columns).

Sister Benedict: *(Chants)* I am an angel sent by God to comfort you, Sister Luke, and to tell you that all your sins are forgiven. The Lord is very pleased with you. He has a place prepared for you at His right hand. Very soon, Sister Luke, I'll take you to Him in Paradise.

(SISTER BENEDICT exits up left).

Sister Luke: Sister Benedict didn't really fool me, but I smiled and stopped screeching and roaring. Because, I could see Sister Benedict's own Guardian Angel shining there beside her and smiling at me too. - It's lovely to be able to see Angels. And Archangels.

(SISTER LUKE takes a page-guimpe from under her chair-copter).

My other story? My father was a schoolteacher up North. Why did he move to the south, you ask. A long story to tell you later. Maybe.

(Lights down)

Stained Glass at Samhain was first presented by Town Hall Productions at the Town Hall Theatre 31 October 2002.

Patricia Burke Brogan is a painter, poet and playwright. Her etchings have won awards at Barcelona and at Listowel. Her publications include *Above the Waves Calligraphy,* poetry (Salmon, 1994) and 2 stage plays, *Eclipsed* (Salmon, 1994) and *Stained Glass at Samhain* (Salmon, 2003). *Eclipsed* has won many awards including a Fringe First at the Edinburgh Theatre Festival 1992 and the USA Moss Hart Award 1994. To date there have been fifty-nine productions of *Eclipsed* on three continents. Patricia received an Arts Council Literature Bursary in 1993 and a European Script Writers' Fund award in 1994. *Requiem of Love,* her new stage play, will be presented in Galway and Dun Laoghaire 2005. Her new collection of poems will be published by Salmon in 2006.

Lorna Shaughnessy

GUADALUPE

We climb the steps
and pin a little miracle to the altar,
a shrunken heart of brass.
Old women open and close their fish mouths,
hands moving around each others' heads,
weaving spells, and fasten
gaudy ribbons at the saint's feet.

We walk along one hundred years
of thankful witness, hand painted
by souls who saw and survived: revolution,
fire, a train crash, open heart surgery;
lives walked in pilgrimage
down the long avenues
named in victorious optimism
to Guadalupe's ochre domes.

In the museum, a bird builds her nest
among coyotes and flowers,
another perches on the patriot priest's shoulder,
and sings about the day a brown saint
met a brown goddess, her feet in the river,
the stars in her mantle
as watchful as the eyes of the dead.

On the trinket seller's stall,
wrapped in the national flag,
Guadalupe smiles down
on dark-skinned cherubs
wearing Indian clothes.

AMONG VOLCANOES

Translation of Pura López Colomé

Born among volcanoes
that appear extinct.
On ground destined to shake.

A shudder. An earthquake.
Someone to-ing and fro-ing
checking if a wall,
a lamp
could come loose and fall
on the sleeping.
We could lose everything.
God willing or not.
Be reduced to a Pompeii.

A naked circumstance
like this winter skylight
has shown me the way
through the fog.
The snow will turn into meltwater
and the light to a denial of fear and atrocity.
The house swallows light on an ancient tongue,
that is heavenly light in the tongue of ancients
and a window here.
The promised land.
True skylight in the darkness.

PENELOPE SINGS FROM THE BEACHES OF ITHACA

Translation of Minerva Margarita Villareal

From this beach I have spent whole nights watching
your bright face.
But your eyes, dark hollows, kept sending me back
to the dead men who set off with him to fight a war
when they were young.
Great mirroring moon. In this darkness, in this
tangle of eternal lament and raw solitude
I declare myself witness to Ulysses' defeats.
I weave forgiveness. The chains of thread have held fast
my rage and protest.
I have always woven on the right side of the cloth,
yet when I turn it over
I find only the loose threads of this story.
And the sea,
the sea
with its fine filigree tormenting my body,
denying the possibility of the nearest kiss.
Ulysses, I have come to loathe your anger
that numbs my desire into submission.
And so I have decided to be silent.
Every stitch a dead word.
There are those who would think I live in forgetfulness
because they cannot hear the cries from my locked room.
Thick walls drown the echoes of my delirium.
I have kept watch more than twenty centuries. Today,
in the murky dawn of this sullied story,
I prepare my ships.

Our Lady of the Lilacs

In the month of Our Lady, I brought
Protestant lilacs to school for the May altar.
My favourite lady lived next door, where
small, sceptered rituals set me apart:
a stool of my own by the hearth,
drinking milk from a china cup.

Later, I sent postcards
from Zanzibar and Chichicastenango
to grace her mantelpiece, confident
my wanderlust would raise a smile,
recalling shared territories of the past,
the thrill of sunsets and palm trees
slotted through the letterbox,
postcards my father sent from hot, farfetched places.

I loved the smell of her powder,
the delicacy of her cheek and her unfading
Church of Ireland choir-singer's voice.
Christmas after Christmas, three perfectly parcelled
flasks of talc for Jim and Kathleen's girls and then,
the widower's voice on the phone

'Gladys is passed away'.

Gladys Heath of number thirty-two Candahar Street,
your church going decency such a part of this place
and yet so rare. In these mis-spelt imperial reaches,
across the Lagan from the 'Holy Land',
the waters of the river never did part,
nor Moses lead us to safer shores.

Drums bear down on Lower Ormeau
as weathered petals fall from your tree
and gather in the faults that split the paving-stones.

SUNDAYS

Apple-tart was baked after Mass,
wincing, we sucked on the bitter cores.
After dinner came Stuart Grainger
all sideburns and britches.

Games of hide and seek meant climbing
into forbidden spaces; the old wardrobe
in the top bedroom up the thirty-two
(obsessively counted) stairs of a house
all high ceilings and landing;
the words bannister and brasses
tripped off our tongues by Primary Two.

Or tying dusters to our feet
and skidding round the kitchen floor.
Sunday tea meant three pickled onions, not two,
and Angie's bravado sandwiches,
banana and salad cream.

Drying the dish from the apple-tart,
I learned the word enamel, found it
tricky on the tongue
'Say enamel animals'
and Mum laughed too,
in all the right places.

BELFAST SCHOOLGIRL'S DIARY, MARCH 22, 1977

God, R.E. was really boring today, Big Mac
cried his mincers out, Philip's brother
got twenty-five years. Good laugh
on the bus after rehearsals, Pamela's party's
tomorrow night, waiting for result
of the vote of no-confidence,
hope Thatcher never gets in.

THREADS

The neighbours must think she's cracked:
a woman in the autumn of her years,
not given to eccentricities, smiles
and hangs dolls' clothing on the line.
Fabrics unseen in twenty-five years,
as vivid now as the flowers she planted in spring.
Paisley was all the rage then, and crocheted capes;
my sisters stitched and hooked sixties *haute couteur*
for the best-dressed dolls in Candahar Street,
each elfin stitch the work of small hands
        and big ideas.

My mother gathers in her multi-coloured harvest,
the steam-iron hisses, strokes away each crease,
fondly teases each pleat and tuck into its rightful place.
Sisters gasp at their own artfulness as names
come flooding back - Tressie, Joyce, Sindy -
all the clan that spanned a good ten years of growing.
I finger the tiny garments and wonder at the scale of their
        perfection.

My belly swells more with each season; early spring,
and friends bring fairy clothes for the coming child,
I hang them on the line, and note
a stitch is called for here and there.

Lorna Shaughnessy was born in Belfast and lives in
Moycullen, Co. Galway. She teaches Spanish at NUI Galway.
Lorna is one of the featured authors in the *Windows
Introductions Series: Writers and Artists* no 6 (2004), she has
published in a variety of literary journals and is currently
translating and editing 2 collections of contemporary Mexican
poetry. She was shortlisted for the Galway County Fireworks
competition for 2005.

Órfhlaith Foyle

Sweet Frankie

Frankie's daddy always promised he'd be where he said he would be. I'll see you in five minutes, half-an-hour, this afternoon or when your mother gets home. Frankie was five years old when he realised other children weren't really hit as much. He kept his mouth shut after too many questions. His teacher, very pretty, very sweet and who also smelled lovely, called him into her office. She gave him two lollipops and he wanted to sit on her knee. He didn't understand the questions she asked him:

'Do you love your mammy and daddy?'

He nodded.

'Does your mammy and daddy love you?'

He nodded again.

'Do they get really angry sometimes?'

Frankie sucked hard on his lollipop. Oh, you really like sweets his teacher said but she looked worried. She bit into her pencil and opened and closed a notebook on her desk. She took the pencil out of her mouth and tried to hum a song. Frankie filled in the words but he kept his voice very quiet, just in case she got angry.

Frankie liked to sing. He liked how big it made him feel. Sometimes he roared songs out of him but always with a pillow in his mouth. Frankie drummed his shoes against the chair he was sitting on. He was getting a little afraid and now he didn't like his teacher anymore. Her smile was all wrong and he didn't believe her when she said if he went out to play now, things would be okay.

That's what she said. Things would be okay now. He made himself repeat it throughout the whole day. He didn't play football in case he forgot the words. He hardly spoke to anyone. He ate his lunch alone and fed some of his sandwich to the ants that crawled across the wooden green table. He screwed his eyes up when he looked at the sun and remembered how his mammy said he would have to ask the nurse to put sunscreen on him.

Frankie put his other sandwich back into his lunch box and went to the sick-room. The nurse had a special smile for him. He handed her the sunscreen and he stood just exactly as he always did when his mammy put it on him. The nurse had different hands and they smelled funny. Her hands were peeling. Frankie saw the tiny bits of skin dangling from her fingers and palm. The nurse upended the bottle into one hand and pounded on the end of the bottle with the other. She asked questions as well.

'So how are you today, Frankie?'

Frankie shrugged his shoulders and winced at the coldness of the sun lotion. The nurse patted her hands over his arm, smiled into his face and then very gently turned his arm this way and that. She did the same to his other arm. Then she crouched down and did the same to his legs, only this time she had to skid a little on her heels to get behind his knees.

'Christ', she said as if something had hurt her.

He started and she put her fingers on his elbow.

'It's okay, Frankie. Just looking at this cut here. Can't let the lotion get into it because it could sting it and make you cry. How did you get that nasty cut?'

His mammy had forgotten to put the plaster on because she had been crying and her face was covered in blisters and Frankie had said nothing; just eaten his cornflakes, drunk his chocolate milk, got his bag and waited outside for his daddy to come out the front door with the car keys and his big voice.

'Come on, Frankie. Time for school'.

In the backseat, Frankie watched the sweat drip onto his dad's shirt collar. After a while his dad pulled at his collar and then undid his tie. Now and again, Frankie could see his daddy look at him in the mirror.

'Okay Frankie?'

'Okay'.

'What are you going to learn today, Frankie?'

'What the teacher says'.

'That's good', said his dad. His dad's eyes flicked and swerved to watch the road. Frankie felt his stomach follow the corners after the car. He has never told his mammy that the car makes him sick. It makes a special kind of hot water come up into his mouth and once he did let it come out but never again. That's what his daddy said; never again and he slung his hand hard across Frankie's head so that colours shot into Frankie's head and the last bit of his sick bubbled down his shirt.

He didn't go to school that day. His father turned the car around and told Frankie to go into his mother and get her to wash his shirt.

'I'll be back in the afternoon. We'll do extra homework to make up for the day'.

Frankie loved his mammy very much. She had red hair that she curled around her fingers as she cooked the meals and she always made sure that Frankie stayed quiet when he was at the table. Frankie knew that without being told but his mammy never stopped telling him it was important.

Frankie was five years old and very sweet. His mammy told him that. Even Mrs Feeney who ran the shop down the street thought so. She'd bend down whenever she saw him, holding her fist out and telling him to choose. He never chose wrong because she always kept sweets in both hands. She'd ruffle her hair, stand up and if Frankie looked up sometimes, instead of looking at the sweets, he would see her face change when she said something to his mother.

'How are you, Anne?'

'Fine. Fine', Frankie's mother would say and move over to the shop counter. 'Frankie, go over and have a look at the comics and eat your sweets. Did you thank Mrs. Feeney?'

'Thanks Mrs. Feeney'.

Frankie loved 'The Incredible Hulk'. The Hulk was big and green and could crush people if he wanted to. He smashed cars and then changed back into being normal. And no one knew who he really was. No one knew who he could magic into.

Frankie sat on the ground, ate his sweets and read a comic. Sometimes Mrs. Feeney gave him a free one. Not all the time. Only when she and his mother had a long talk and if Mrs. Feeney looked like she had cried. Then she was extra kind. Then she would bend down and kiss Frankie on the cheek and say what a sweet, lovely boy he was and wouldn't he always watch out for his mammy?

Frankie couldn't always do that.

Sometimes he would be too tired and fall asleep only to wake up and hear his mammy screaming. He'd hear her being slammed into things and he knew not to get up out of bed because she didn't want that. The last time he'd gone to help her, she had yelled at him to go back into his room and his father stood with her hair in his fists, because he was holding her head up and she looked like a doll.

Other times, Frankie's daddy would come back when he said he would and be kind. He'd bring back something nice like flowers and chocolates and they'd all eat them instead of food. Afterwards they'd watch something on the television and then Frankie would be told to go to bed and later there would be no sound. Nothing at all. Frankie would have to press his ear very close to his parents' bedroom door before he'd hear something that sounded like a frightened animal.

Frankie's daddy believed in turning up when he said he would. Frankie learned that from him. Frankie learned it was good manners to smile, look neat and turn up when you were supposed to. Frankie never finished all of his food on his plate and sometimes he only shaved off a little with his knife and then onto his fork and that was all he would eat. His daddy said he would get hungry soon enough.

Frankie began to feed the birds as well as the ants. He preferred birds and he knew The Hulk could be very kind to baby things so he was too. He didn't like the noise of the playground and so he just sat with the birds.

It was his daddy's belt-buckle that made the cut on the back of his knee. His daddy had put his mother's head under the hot tap in the kitchen and shoved his body against her legs to make her stop kicking. Frankie heard her voice scream in gaps: first water, then her scream, then a funny mixture of them both, like singing bubbles.

Frankie tried to save his mammy. He ran into his daddy's legs and bit them through their trousers. He bit enough to feel blood come into his mouth. His daddy screamed and tried to shake Frankie off but Frankie bit harder. Frankie felt his chest grow big inside him as if something was trying to get out. He bit and bit and bit. His daddy's hands tried to pull Frankie's head away but Frankie imagined how The Hulk would not let go so neither would he.

His daddy got his fingers into the sides of Frankie's mouth and prised his jaw apart. Frankie remembered later on how there was just silence in the room until his daddy struggled to stand and then went out of the room.

'Wait there. I'll be back in a minute'.

Frankie stood with blood dribbling down his chin. He looked at his mammy who was crying with no sound. Her face was pressed against the sink cupboard. It was red and angry and she tried to cover it with her hair.

Frankie could hear his daddy coming back down the hall so Frankie spat out the blood in his mouth. His daddy came into the kitchen with his belt wrapped over his fist.

'This is what you get', he said.

The nurse put a plaster on the cut and made a phone call. She spoke for a long time and now and again smiled over at Frankie. When she finished talking into the phone, she asked him would he like a juice and he said he'd like an orange one.

'Look what I also have for you, Frankie'. She gave him a piece of chocolate from her handbag and also some pens to colour in a picture book. After a while, Frankie's teacher came in to see the nurse but she smiled at Frankie first. She said his daddy was here to take him home. Frankie put down his pens and the last square of chocolate but the nurse said he could eat that up. Before he went out the door, the nurse crouched down to look into his eyes and said:

'You know Frankie, you shouldn't be getting those kinds of cuts at all'.

Frankie nodded and the nurse stood up, reached up to a shelf and gave him a red lollipop that had been in a pile of lollipops. His teacher brought him out to his daddy who was sitting on the long low bench outside the staff room. His daddy was smiling and took Frankie by the hand and told him to say goodbye to his teacher. Had he all his books?

'Good ... Goodnight Miss Hanlon'.

'Goodnight Mr. Folan. Goodnight Frankie'.

Sometimes Frankie imagined his teacher calling him Sweet Frankie as well.

Órfhlaith Foyle was born in Nigeria to Irish missionary parents and lived in Kenya and Malawi before emigrating to Australia, where she received a BA in Humanities. She now lives in Galway. Her work has been widely published and her first novel *Belios* (Lilliput) is published this year and launched at the Cúirt International Festival of Literature in Galway.

Rose Tuelo Brock

MY COMPANION

You turned, stared, open-mouthed.
Quite.
I myself, am in constant consternation,
How a frame so small,
could be loaded with so much behind.
A wobbling companion ever-following,
surely making its presence felt.

I have tried starvation, swimming, skipping,
Walking, running, to rid myself of it.
Still, it is there. As if to say:
'You are going nowhere without me'
Like a camel's hump, I am stuck with it.

Perhaps I should be living in the Kalahari
Walking miles searching for sustenance
Carrying babies to the dozen,
on my well disposed steatopygia.

I suppose, lest I get ideas,
with my colouring and my behind
Mother Africa follows me
to keep me well grounded.

THE WOMAN ON THE BUS

Breathlessly, I boarded the bus.
As I handed him the fare,
I begged the driver to warn me
when the bus came close to my stop.
He did not want to know.

Sat by the window,
I kept my stare at the route, to make sure.
Opposite me, she smiled generously.
It relaxed me enough to smile back.

'Where do you wish to get off, love?'
I explained.
'Not to worry;
I'll be getting off there myself'.
So, at Clery's, we both alighted.

She came closer:
'Those earrings, how beautiful.
Is that the shape of Africa?'
she asked.
'*Yes Ma'am*', I beamed back.
'A lovely part of this world;
You are most welcome here',
she added.
I thanked her.
We smiled and said our goodbyes.

Does she even know what 'play' means?
At four, she had to mind her baby brother,
as her mother worked in the rice fields
and father lay coughing all day and night.

At six, she went to work,
packing tobacco into paper tubes.
For that, she took home a small coin
not enough to buy herself a meal.
She developed a cough which was to be
her lifelong companion.

At eight, the landlord decided
She was big enough to do some real work
Bent over for hours picking tea leaves,
and carrying loaded bags on her still-to-grow back.
For that, she took home a child's wage
Not enough for the daily rice meal for the family.

At ten, her mother was exhausted
and her father finally gave up the ghost.
So, she had to be the bread earner.
At twelve, a second-hand man eyed her.
Took her away, to be his wife,
he said!

Rose Tuelo Brock (née Leteane) was born in South Africa.
She taught science in high schools in Zimbabwe, Kenya, and
Lesotho. She, her husband and two sons arrived in Galway in
early 1979. In 1986 she completed a Diploma in Community
Development in UCG. Rose was a founder member of the
Galway One World Centre. She has written essays and given
talks on Human Rights issues and related subjects. She writes
a regular column in Galway's *City Tribune*, and short stories
and verse with hopes of getting published.

ONCE I WAS A CHILD

Once I was a child and I believed in God, scapulars, fairies and bogeymen.

It was nineteen fifty-four, the Marian year, and everyone in Ireland believed in God and scapulars. There were processions, thousands of them, the length and breadth of the country. There was Knock and there was magic.

It was the Marian year and I believed my harassed mother when she told me a birth cert was a piece of paper with your name, age and address written on it. So I wrote my own birth cert on a scrap of paper, to satisfy Sister Celsis, who insisted there could be no Communion without a cert and there would be no going on to second class if you hadn't made your First. Frank Sinatra belted it out for us, 'You can't have one, ... without the other!' He wasn't singing about the Irish church and state, of course, for Frank was an American and he didn't know a thing about Ireland.

Anyway, in I marched and handed Sister Celsis my certificate, as she stood talking to Sister Aloysius; well, they laughed and laughed and laughed. Children were a great source of entertainment in those days.

I still believed in God after I made my Communion, although I did have doubts. 'If God is so good' I reasoned, 'why is there evil in the world?' But this was pre-Vatican Two and if it wasn't in the Penny Catechism you didn't ask. I gave up asking questions afterwards.

I discovered failure when I was seven and they asked me to sing *Adeste Fidelis*. It was Christmas and money was short and families had to make their own entertainment. De Valera had great time for church and family. Everyone knew he was doing his best for families, for the whole country, in fact, but what with industry stagnating, a balance of payments deficit, and all the rest of it, well, things weren't going so well. The whole 'comely maidens dancing at the cross-roads' thing hadn't worked out either, for all the youth were emigrating to Britain. Anyway, I sang like a nightingale, and they laughed until they cried.

Children were a great source of entertainment in those days. I gave up singing afterwards. I gave up believing in fairies and bogeymen around the same time, but this being Ireland, God took longer.

I discovered love when I was eight. 'Gran, why are you crying?' I asked. 'Because I'm going to die' the old woman sighed, driven to distraction, childminding, her husband working beyond in Scotland; her daughter, mother of twelve, aged thirty, up in Vincent's getting her varicose veins done. 'Don't cry, Gran', I said, 'I love you, Gran, don't die'. 'I won't die, hen', she said and dried her eyes.

I discovered treachery when I was nine. These were the Whitaker years, when Dev was told he'd have to give up his economic dream. 'You'll have to give up that dream, Eamon', Ken warned, 'open up to multinationals, otherwise it's down the tubes!' 'Did you know your Gran is going to die?' the aunts ask slyly, not caring a hoot about the economy, as, eyes narrowed, they watched and waited for the tears to flow to order, which they did, out of a sad empty well.

Children were a great source of entertainment in those days. I gave up love afterward.

I discovered sex when I was ten - a little late, but then this was Ireland - not the real thing, just a few bare facts from a medical book. I was only doing a bit of research, of course, for it was a well-known fact that there was no sex in Ireland before television. Except we found out later there was sex in Ireland before television, lots and lots of it: up and down the country, in orphanages, reformatories, vestries, convents, no end to it. But it was all very discreet, I certainly didn't know a thing about it at the time.

But as I said, children were a great source of entertainment in those days.

A lot of them gave up sex afterwards.

Nineteen hundred and sixty and the world economy was booming. Welfare meant better standards of living for all and everyone was challenging the system and the received wisdom. But that was abroad and in America. Things weren't moving quite so fast in Ireland, where we were still managing to hold onto traditional values: censorship, sexual repression, that sort of thing. In any case, I was developing my own brand of wisdom.

By nineteen sixty-six, the year the IRA blew up Nelson's Pillar, I had a map for life under my belt that didn't include involvement in things that were none of my business, such as the North, feminism, civil rights or student protests and since marriage had to be achieved somewhere between age twenty and twenty six, I kept my eye on the ball.

After the nuptials were signed, I threw away my map and followed my man's, which prescribed unusual hobbies like DIY, restoration of antiques and building walls. I did my best, but boredom and *ennui* set in and eventually, I found I couldn't follow his map at all; I got lost. Everyone agreed I lacked a plan.

When I found myself again, I was no longer a child and I knew there was no God, no map, no plan. I began writing my own plan. These developments brought their own problems, of course. It was nineteen eighty-six and from the pulpit, the bishops had just won a victory against the introduction of divorce into Ireland. The Church were still hankering after the days when men were men, women were women, and children were a great source of entertainment.

Once I was a child and I believed in God, scapulars, fairies and bogeymen. Now I am a woman and I don't believe in any of those things, anymore.

CALLING THE TUNE

The thirtysomething sylph
slipping through couturier skirts and tops
invites her bored husband to judge.

An indifferent yawn and shrug
become a grin of instant pleasure
when offered a cup of Maxwell House.

In order to prolong the kick
he indicates silk lingerie
to his gorgeous anorexic spouse.

An apparition in red, a kiss mouthed
as coffee, sex and sale meet
in the high street Dublin boutique.

Kraft consortium purchase beans
at fourteen cents a kilo
from indigenous anorexic people.

We shake the day out before us
like a linen tablecloth, a gift,
reserved for a special affair such as this.

Measuring highs in dun envelopes,
dressing hours in black lace,
milking Larkin* for misogyny.

Without warning I stumble awkwardly.
You turn a light on my space
and observe a grubby stain spread.

I crumble - over tea and rye cake,
bewildered by the myriad ways
we clearly no longer fit.

*Philip Larkin, poet

Maureen Gallagher was born in Monaghan. She lives in
Galway where she works as a special needs resource teacher.
Her poetry and short stories have been published widely in
Ireland, Britain, New Zealand, Canada, the United States and
broadcast on RTÉ. Her criticism won her a prize in the New
Writer essay competition. A selection of her poetry is
included in *Anthology 1*. She featured in the 2004 Poetry
Ireland Introductions readings and is a nominee for the 2005
Hennessy Poetry Award.

Susan Bennett

The Messenger

He enjoyed the work, although he knew that most of his friends wondered why he did it. They thought he was daft to get up so early every day, to stick with a job which was physically hard work, often spending most of the day outside, in this city known for its driving rain and the cold wind that came off the sea. This morning was dry, though the early sun tried and failed to warm the city, and he was more than content as he cycled down the narrow streets to the old grey and red-bricked building which stood on one of the more accessible main streets near the city centre But he preferred this route through the back lanes because they were quiet at this time of the day. Later, it would be different.

He could choose any one of a number of routes to work - they all took him downhill towards the river, away from the smoky estates which covered the hills on the north side of the city. He remembered as a child freewheeling down this very lane most Saturday mornings, with Ed on the seat behind him as he stood on the pedals, hurtling down towards the market near the Post Office. He remembered no fear of his own, just a feeling of speed and Ed's long skinny arms holding tight around his waist. Was it only a few years ago? Now eleven, his brother Ed considered himself too old for hanging around with his big brother and preferred to keep to the company of his mates. He realised suddenly that he saw very little of the younger boy now. And he himself had changed, had grown up, had gotten over the need to get everywhere quickly, instead enjoying the journey itself and, especially on these fresh winter mornings, no longer speeding down towards the river. He loved the fresh look of the streets early in the day with so few people about, and the notion of a city just beginning to shake the sleep off itself. He liked the malty smell of the brewery on the damp air near the river and the feeling of almost being the first to discover the streets every morning.

Things had been difficult for a while, and he recalled the day he'd come home with the news of the job. His mother was at the sink in the back kitchen and as he passed round the side of the house, she'd seen him and smiled out through the small window which faced onto the yard, welcoming him home as she had every day since he'd first gone out in the world.

He was the man in the house now that his father was gone, forced away from home by the need to earn a wage, he supposed. She never spoke to him about it and he didn't ask. Once he'd heard Ellen - at six the youngest of them - ask her mother where Dada was, and when was he coming back? But he'd gone out of the room and climbed the narrow stairs, unable to bear the possibility of hearing the truth. That day as he came through the back door dipping his head to avoid the low door lintel, his Mam had wiped her hands on her apron before closing the door behind him, telling him to sit down while she got him something to eat.

'How was school?' she asked, putting the kettle on the hob, then lighting the gas ring underneath it.

'I don't know Mam' he replied, 'I didn't go in today'.

He waited, afraid because he knew that this wasn't going to be easy for her. As she turned towards him, he saw the determination in her face and feared the worst.

'Listen to me', he said quickly, for once filling the silence with his earnestness. 'I've got a job. The money's okay, I'm to start at 6.30 in the morning but I'll be finished before teatime and every Sunday off'. She sat down suddenly and looked directly at him.

'Where? Don't tell me it's in Duggan's'.

Duggan's Factory was the biggest employer on this side of the city and he knew she had firm views about any of her family working there. Neighbours had gone in as young men, worked hard and long, then ended up on the scrap-heap when that same hard work and long hours left them unable to carry on. More recently, there had been an attempt to unionise the workers and there were stories of discrimination by the employers against those seen as troublemakers. She wanted no part of it for her family - especially not for him. He knew that she wanted him to do better than working in Duggan's, to finish school and get a real job - not like those her brothers and uncles had, but a job away from the factories and the railways, into an office or a schoolroom. He'd had such ambitions once himself but now that his father was no longer around, he couldn't bear to see her struggle to manage. He saw her constant battle to feed and clothe five children younger than himself, to keep them warm and out of trouble. He saw that she had no time or energy to smile or laugh, or to sing as she used to do when he was younger, and on some days no energy even to talk. And he knew that whatever money she received from his father at intervals and where ever it came from (sometimes the Midlands, sometimes further north, once even from London), it was not sufficient to keep body and soul together. Once again he fought back the silent resentment and frustration that so often threatened to rise up and choke him. Still, without that money he didn't know how they'd manage and although it was irregular, he supposed it meant that the man hadn't completely abandoned them.

'No, it's not Duggan's', he said and stood up. Although they were close, physical contact wasn't part of their relationship now having somehow stopped long ago when he had started to grow. Now he put his arms around her awkwardly and pulled her to him. 'Don't worry Mam', he said, looking down and trying to reassure her, to divert her resistance. 'It will be all right'.

He noticed with a shock just how slight she was, felt her thin shoulders against his chest and knew for the first time in his entire life that rather than being her eldest son, he was now a grown man.

Forcing the memory from his mind and with both hands on the brakes, he held the bike from rushing downhill, enjoying this morning's journey in the cool winter air. His mother had resigned herself in the face of his determination, and he knew she was relieved at the regular wage coming into the house. The job was okay but the high point of each day was the journey there every morning. Later - weary from travelling around the city - he would slowly trudge back up the hill towards home, getting off the bicycle when he couldn't physically push himself any further. On good days the journeys around the city were mostly on the south side - which was flatter - sometimes as far out as the Golf Club, to big new houses with proper gardens and driveways. Some mornings when he'd just got to work, he'd had to cycle straight back up the hill - sometimes even beyond his own estate. On those days if he could, he used to call home during the day for something to eat - standing at the kitchen sink in his uniform, refusing to sit or dawdle while he was on duty. He knew it broke up the day for her, and he had never come home to find her doing anything other than working, trying to make ends meet and keep the home clean and warm for the younger ones coming in from school. But she always chatted with him, and liked to hear about the trips he'd taken that morning. Of course, she never asked him for details - Mr Phelan was very stern on the subject of the confidentiality of the mails. Just once though, in the early days, she had asked him if he brought good news telegrams and well as the other kind, and he had exaggerated a little to reassure her that all was not as bleak as it might be with the world outside.

When he reached the main street this morning, he looked up to his left and checked the time shown on the giant white-faced clock over Harding's, the Mens' Outfitters. Seeing it was only twenty after the hour, he relaxed. He didn't understand how some of the other lads could race into the yard at the very last minute, throwing their bikes up against the wall and running into the building through the big oak door which led from the yard. He took the job and the work seriously, turning up on time and wearing his uniform with some pride, although the dark green jacket and pants were a little too big, having been left by a previous lad who only stuck at the job until the weather turned. In the early days he'd been embarrassed to meet his friends around the city, as they lounged against the river wall or waited to whistle out the girls from the factories. But in time he'd gotten used to them and they'd left off ribbing him soon enough.

As he walked across the back hall, he saw that Mr Phelan was already inside. The first morning he'd come down the hill to work, he'd miscalculated the time and arrived far too early - well before six o'clock. But Mr Phelan was already in the sorting room at that time, and had brought him in and shown him how things were run. The old man was always there before any of the other employees, and didn't leave until they'd all collected their things and gone home every evening. Sometimes he wondered where Mr Phelan lived, and if he had a wife and family - maybe even a son like himself. Although some of the other lads made fun of Phelan behind his back, the boy thought he was okay. He supposed the older man had worked at the Post Office for many years, and had seen lots of young fellas like him come and go.

He was strict about things like the uniform, and the care of their bicycles, and got angry if you were late or didn't return promptly from every delivery. Phelan knew the distances across the whole of the city, and there was no point trying to fool him with stories about accidents or punctures, or delays of any kind. He made it clear that the delivery of telegrams was a serious business, and that working for the Post Office was something of which one should be proud, carrying on a tradition of service that had been in existence since man first identified a need to communicate with others who were some distance away. He knew that Mr Phelan saw the Post Office as a service at the forefront of progress, an institution separate from the people it was trying to serve. He didn't differentiate between the post men, who were mostly older men, and the young messenger boys who delivered the telegrams. Months before and just days after he'd started the job, the boy had come back to the sorting room to hear the older man scolding one of the other messengers for some misdemeanour, some failure of duty or other. There were rumours among the others but no-one knew the details of what offence had been committed, and shortly after the lecture the culprit had left the employment of the service. That evening before they left for home, Mr Phelan had taken the opportunity to remind the remaining lads and the post-men of the rules of engagement and, so stern was his tone, that not one of them questioned him or jostled each other while he spoke. Instead they stood and listened, then quietly hung up their caps and uniforms before saying good night to the old man and going out into the yard to make their separate ways home in the fading light.

Now as he came into the sorting room from a short easy delivery to a solicitor's office just over the river, Mr Phelan looked up. The boy had noticed earlier that the old man looked tired. Rheumy eyes in his pale face made him seem suddenly older and he had turned away from the boy after perfunctorily greeting him that morning. At the time he had wondered briefly if the man was unwell, then had collected his uniform from the row of pegs near the stove, and went to get dressed for work. With his mind on the work he had to do, he hadn't given it any further thought until now. As he reported for the next delivery, the older man stepped towards him and gripped his arm with his free left hand. Startled by the sudden physical contact, the boy stood stock still.

'I'm sorry, son', Mr Phelan said, holding out his right hand in which he held, as usual, a small white stiff envelope. The boy reached out automatically and took the telegram from his boss.

'Take your time', he heard the old man say before he turned away.

He looked down and saw from the postmark that it had come from Manchester. That was in the west of England, wasn't it? The stiff white envelope was addressed to his mother, at the house he'd only left a couple of hours previously. He felt the room go quiet.

The wintry sun slanted through the small window at the back of the house, and landed in a dragged out square of pale yellow on the floor. Standing still, her wet hands - red and sore now from years of work - rested on the edge of the ceramic sink. Looking down at them, she slowly flexed the stiff fingers and turned her hands over to look at the palms. She wondered where her soft white hands had gone - the ones she'd been so proud of as a younger woman. She surprised herself with this small vanity then started as she heard a knock and the rattle of the loose pane of glass in the front door. She turned and out of habit, stepped over the square of light on the floor before drying her hands on her wrap and opening the door into the hall. Probably some salesman, she thought.

The short narrow space was cluttered with the debris of a growing family. A doll's pram blocked most of the width of the hall, and a child's scooter lay beneath it forcing her to hitch her skirt slightly at the knee to step over it. The only light here was unnaturally yellow, coming through two mismatched glass panes in the door. Although they'd only lived here a year, she'd had to replace both panes at one time or another. Well, after school the children liked to play ball or chasing on the small square of grass outside and she liked to have them near her, not roaming the streets like some of her neighbours' kids.

She could see the shape of a man through the left hand pane of yellow bubble glass. He was taller than her although the view through the glass was distorted, and meant that she couldn't tell if he was facing her or looking back down the hill towards the city. The few callers she'd had often did that, apparently surprised by the sudden sight of the river and city straggled below them once they'd turned their backs to the house. She'd open the door to find them searching the view for familiar landmarks, like the church steeple, or the main bridge across the river. With her hand on the latch she hesitated for a second, then opened the door. He turned at once and took off his uniform cap. Misunderstanding at first, she opened the door fully and stood back to let him into the hall, wondering why he'd come to the front rather than making his own way around the back of the house as usual. But he stood where he was. Only when he held out the small stiff envelope towards her, did she understand.

Susan Bennett: If you ask where she's from, you'll get a range of answers. Born in Dublin, one time resident of Limerick, the Midlands, Dublin (again and again), she now lives between the mysteries of the Burren and the wonder of the Atlantic. She describes herself as a contented middle-aged pen-pusher with no angst or trauma to report, other than what life throws at her.

TUIGE MISE?

'Tá tá chun í a phósadh, mar sin ...'

'Is dócha go bhfuilim ...'

'Tusa ... ag pósadh! Ní thig liom é a chreidiúint'.

'Hmm, tá sé deacair é a chreidiúint, ceart go leor'.

'Ach tusa, thar éinne eile, a Phaidí tá sé dochreidte!'

'Bhuel, níl an tarna rogha agam, anois agus í ag iompar'.

'Tusa id dhaidí! Sin rud eile nach féidir liom a shamhlú go héasca'.

'Ná mise ach oiread'.

'Beidh cailíní na cathrach seo croíbhriste! Níl aon dabht faoi sin'.

'Ha'.

'Bhuel, a Phaidí, *fair play* dhuit, níl a fhios agamsa cén chaoi a ndéanann tú é. Ag rith timpeall leis na cailíní go léir agus fós fanann Cathy dílis duit. Agus í lán-tsásta thú a phósadh!'

'*Na cailíní go léir*! Éirigh as, a Tony. Ní bhíonn thar bheirt in éineacht agamsa riamh'.

'An ag magadh atá tú? Céard faoin samhradh sin go raibh tú ag rith timpeall leis na *twins* fionna úd ó Bhaile Átha Cliath i ngan fhios do Cathy? Agus níor leor duine amháin acu duit, bhí ort luí leis an mbeirt acu!'

'Aaaa, bhí sin difriúil ar fad'.

'Ó, an raibh, muise?'

'Bhuel, nach rabhadar díreach cosúil lena chéile -ní rabhasa ábalta idirdhealú a dhéanamh eatarthu ar chor ar bith'.

'Ó, leithscéal an-mhaith é sin! Sea, thaitneodh sin le Cathy'.

'Dia dhíbh a chailíní!'

'Dia dhuit, a Phaidí, cén chaoi a bhfuil tú?'

'Maith go leor, maith go leor - ach go bhfuilim préachta leis an bhfuacht ó bheith im sheasamh amuigh anseo. Tá sibh araon ag breathnú go hálainn anocht, bail ó Dhia oraibh!'

'Go raibh maith agat!'

'A Phaidí, chualamar go bhfuil tú féin agus Cathy geallta. Comhghairdeas!'

'Go raibh maith agat, a Shíle, bhuel, ní féidir liom fanacht i mo bhaitsiléir go deo, is dócha'.

'Ha, ha! Bhuel, guím gach rath ar an mbeirt agaibh!'

'Dia leat, a stór. Bíodh oíche dheas agaibh anois'.

'Slán go fóill, a Phaidí'.

'Slán!'

'Huh, cheapas féin go mbeifeá-sa id bhaitsiléir go deo, a Phaidí. *The oldest swinger in town* - mar a déarfá!'

'Measaim gur agatsa a bheas an onóir sin fós, a Tony!'

'Dia dhíbh!'

'Dia dhíbh!'

'Dia is Muire dhíbh!'

'Dia ár réiteach! An bhfaca tú na cosa fúithi sin!'

'Ba mhaith an sás í sin chun tú a théamh sa leaba oíche fhuar!'

'Dia dhuit, a Phaidí!'

'Dia is Muire dhuit, a Debbie!'

'Cén chaoi a bhfuil tú?'

'Ó, ag strácáil liom, a Debbie, ag strácáil liom...'

'*Hi*, a Phaidí!'

'*Hi*, a Mháirín ... tá sibh beirt ag breathnú go hálainn, mar is gnách!'

'Ó, an béal bán! Níor chaill tú riamh é, a Phaidí'.

'An bhfuil sé fíor go bhfuil tú féin agus Cathy geallta?'

'Tá, muise'.

'Ó ... Comhghairdeas'.

'Comhghairdeas, a Phaidí! Is iontach an scéal é sin'.

'Go raibh maith agaibh. Bainigí taitneamh as an oíche'.

'Feicfimid thú i Vaja's i gcomhair caife níos deanaí, b'fhéidir?'

'Le cuidiú Dé, muna gcaillfear mé leis an bhfuacht'.

'Ba chóir dhuit do chuid *thermals* a chaitheamh'.

'Caithfidh mé cuimhneamh air sin an chéad oíche eile. Oíche mhaith agaibh!'

'Oíche mhaith!'

'Dia ár réiteach, nach tusa an slíomadóir ceart, a Phaidí. *Tá sibh beirt ag breathnú go hálainn, mar is gnách!* Níl aon teora leat'.

'Ní foláir bheith deas béasach leis na cailíní, a Tony. Sin riail uimhir a haon'.

'Aaaa, anois, nílimse inchurtha leatsa ar chor ar bith, a mhac! Ní haon Romeo mise. Ó a dhiabhail, sea chugainn an Fear Mór arís ...'

'Bhuel, a leaids? Aon trioblóid ó shin?'

'Blas ar bith, a Sheáin, gach aon rud breá ciúin ó shin'.

'Go maith. Gabh i leith, a Tony, ná bí chomh trodach leis na custaiméirí as seo amach, an gcloiseann tú mé?

'Ní rabhas ach im chosaint féin!'

'Ceart go leor, ceart go leor ... Nílim ach a' rá, bígí cúramach, ar son Dé. Caithfimid troid agus bruíon a sheachaint anseo! *Okay?*'

'*Okay*, a Sheáin, coimeádfaidh mise srian air'.

'Maith an fear, a Phaidí! A dhiabhail, tá sé fuar amuigh anseo. Rachaidh mé isteach arís ...'

'... Ar chuala tú riamh a leithéid? 'Chríost! Céard ba chóir dom a dhéanamh agus triúr meisceoir ag bagairt orainn!'

'Aaaa, anois a Tony, chuaigh tú an-dian ar mo dhuine an uair sin, agus tá a fhios agat go maith é'.

'Agus ceard faoi féin? Nach bhfaca tú é a m' ionsaí?

'Níor ghá dhuit é a leagadh, más ea'.

'Agus seans a thabhairt dó mise a leagadh, an ea?'

'Ní raibh sin i gceist aige ar chor ar bith'.

'Rinne sé iarracht dul tharam!'

'Agus má rinne féin, níor ghá duit é a leagadh'.

'Dúirt muid leo nach raibh cead isteach acu mar go raibh siad ar meisce ach níor ghlacadar leis'.

'Níor ghá dhuit é a leagadh'.

'Ó, éirigh as! Nílimid go léir chomh bog leatsa, a Phaidí'.

'Tarraingeoidh an racht feirge sin trioblóid ort, a Tony, táim á rá leat'.

'Bhuel, b'fhearr liomsa an fód a sheasamh agus gan bheith i mo mheatachán!'

'Dia dhuit, a Phaidí!'

'Dia dhíbh, a chailíní! Cén chaoi a bhfuil sibh?'

'Táimid go maith, go raibh maith agat'.

'Níl tú chun muidne a bhac, an bhfuil, a Phaidí?'

'Mise? Ní dhéanfainnse feall mar sin oraibhse!'

'Maith thú! Slán!'

'Slán go fóill, a chailíní!'

'A Phaidí, in ainm Dé, céard tá ort? Ní rabhadar sin ach a cúig déag nó a sé déag!'

'Tá a fhios agam. Ach tá siad sa rang agam thuas sa scoil agus beidh an cigire chugam an tseachtain sea chugainn, dá bhrí sin caithfidh mé bheith deas leo ionas go mbeidh siad deas ciúin an lá sin. An dtuigeann tú leat mé?'

'Nach tú an rógaire! Bhuel, má fhaigheann Seán amach gur scaoil tú isteach iad, díolfaidh tú as. Seans go gcaillfidh tú do jab dá bharr'.

'Is cuma sa diabhal liomsa faoin jab suarach seo - i mo sheasamh amuigh sa bhfuacht an oíche go léir. Tá an *Dip* i bhfad níos tábhachtaí - táim á rá leat. 'Chríost! Éist liomsa, táim ag caint díreach cosúil lem mháthair'.

'Bhuel, buntáiste eile a bhaineann leis an múinteoireacht - na cailíní scoile go léir. Taitníonn cailíní scoile go mór leatsa, a mhac!'

'Taitníonn *chuile* shórt cailín liomsa, a Tony, mar is eol duit'.

'Agus ag trácht ar chailíní scoile, cén chaoi a bhfuil Bridie?'

'Bridie? Ó, tá Bridie togha'.

'Gabh i leith, an bhfuil sí go maith sa leaba, an bhfuil?'

'Bhuel, tá sí óg agus gan mórán cleachtadh, tá a fhios agat, ach ag an am céanna ...'

'Múinfidh tusa go leor di, gan amhras!'

'Go díreach!'

'Táimse in éad leat. Is cailín breá í sin!'

'Tá sí deas, ceart go leor'.

'Agus níl tuairim faoin spéir ag Cathy faoi Bhridie fós?'

'Níl. Agus níl sí chun é a fháil amach má choinníonn chuile dhuine a chlab dúnta, nach fíor dhom, a Tony?'

'Bhuel, is féidir leat brath ormsa, ar aon nós. Tá a fhios agat go maith nach sceithfinnse ort. Ach gabh i leith, céard faoi Aindriú?'

'Céard faoi?'

'Níl a fhios aige fós, mar sin?'

'An dóigh leatsa go mbeadh aon bhaint ag Aindriú liomsa dá mbeadh a fhios aige go rabhas ag luí lena chailín ionúin?'

'Is dócha nach mbeadh. 'Chríost, a Phaidí, dá ndéanfása feall mar sin ormsa mharóinn thú!'

'Ná bí buartha, níor chuireas aon dúil in aon chailín a bhí agatsa riamh, a Tony, bhíodar ró-ghránna'.

'*Feck off!* ... Bhí go leor cailíní deasa agamsa'.

'Cé bhí, mar shampla?'

'Bhuel ... em ... Fan go bhfeicfidh mé ... Oooo, breathnaigh cé atá chugainn ... an bheirt chéanna ... Bridie-an-*babe* agus Aindriú-an-t-Aineolaí!'

'Shshsh ... Tony, dún do chlab, maith an fear ...'

'*Hi* ...'

'*Hi* a Phaidí'.

'*Hi*, a Bhridie, nach tusa atá ag breathnú go deas anocht'.

'Go raibh maith agat'.

'*Hey*, Aindriú ... an bhfuil an deich bpunt sin agat dom fós?'

'Em ... níl ... brón orm. Dé Luain, okay? Beidh sé agam Dé Luain'.

'Ceart go leor. Oíche mhaith agaibh!'

'Oíche mhaith, a Phaidí'.

'... Tá an cailín sin splanctha id dhiaidh, a Phaidí'.

'Meas tú?'

'Gan dabht ar bith! An chaoi ar bhreathnaigh sí ort ansin. Cuireann sé iontas orm nach dtugann Aindriú tada faoi deara'.

'Tá mo dheartháirín dúr agus dall. Tá sé chomh mór sin i ngrá léi nach gcreideann sé go bhféadfadh sí fiú amháin breathnú ar aon fhear eile ... Ach is cuma anois. Táim tar éis a rá léi go bhfuil deireadh lenár gcaidreamh agus sin sin'.

'Ar mhaithe le Cathy?'

'Ar mhaithe le chuile dhuine. D'éirigh an scéal róchasta ar fad. Shíleas nach mbeadh ann ach píosa spraoi - *one night stand*, mar a déarfá. Ní raibh mé ag súil leis go mbeadh a thuilleadh uaithi'.

'Aaa, caithfear díol as bheith i do stail sa leaba, a mhac! Éiríonn na mná cíocrach'.

'Gabh i leith, Tony, féach ar an gcarr sin'.

'Níl cead isteach an bealach seo, dar ndóigh'.

'Táid dallta, déarfainn'.

'Agus an luas atá faoi ...'

'Tá sé ag tabhairt aghaidh orainn ... Bhfuil aithne agat -'

'Céard sa diabhal ...?'

'*FUCK YOUS!*'

'A Phaidí. A Phaidí! An bhfuil tú *alright?* A PHAIDÍ!'

'Céard a tharla?'

'A Phaidí. A Phaidí. Dúisigh ... Dúisigh ... A Phaidí! *Oh fuck* ... HEY! DUINE ÉlGIN! Fóir orm! Fóir orm!'

'Céard a tharla do mo dhuine?'

'PAIDÍ. PAIDÍ. DÚISIGH, AR SON DÉ, DÚISIGH!'

'An bhfuil sé *alright?*'

'Paidí! An gcloiseann tú mé? Ó, 'Chríost! Ná seasaigí timpeall ag breathnú air. Tusa, isteach leat go beo agus cuir na *bouncers* eile amach chugainn ar an dtoirt!'

'*Okay*'.

'A Phaidí, an gcloiseann tú mé? Ó, in ainm Dé, a Phaidí, abair rud éigin!'

'-A Tony? Céard a tharla?'

'A Sheáin, tá Paidí gortaithe! Caitheadh cloch leis ... thit sé i bhfanntais ... Tá sé gan aithne gan urlabhra ...'

'Tom ... Isteach leat go beo agus cuir glaoch ar otharcharr!'

'*Right, Boss*'.

'Carr ... Tháinig carr, chaith duine éigin cloch linn ... Bhuail an chloch Paidí sa chloigeann ...'

'Tóg bog é, a Tony, beidh sé togha. Tá otharcharr ar an mbealach anois. Beidh gach rud togha. Gabh i leith ... cuir an cóta seo faoina chloigeann ...'

'Tharla chuile rud chomh sciobtha sin... Ní raibh seans aige. .. ní raibh seans ar bith aige ...'

'Tóg go réidh e, a Tony ... beidh sé ceart go leor...'

Rugadh **Tina Nic Enrí** gcathair na Gaillimhe i 1969. Bhain sí céim amach sa Bhéarla agus sa Ghaeilge i gColáiste na hOllscoile Gaillimh agus ansin céim Máistreachta sa Scríbhneoireacht Chruthaitheach in Ollscoil Mhanchain. Chaith sí tréimhsí ag obair i Londain, i Manchain agus i Madrid. Fuair Tina aitheantas mar scribhneaoir óg ag scríobh trí mheán na Gaeilge nuair a bhronn Uachtarán na hÉireann, Máire Mhic Ghiolla Íosa Gradam Seachtain na Gaeilge uirthi i 1998. Bronnadh Gradam Duais Liteartha an Oireachtais ar an úrscéal - *Tuige Mise?* - a d'fhoilsigh Coiscéim - i 2002. Foilsíodh a céad úrscéal: *An Coimhthíoch Caol Dubh* (Coiscéim) i 1994. Cuireadh an leabhar seo ar shiollabas na Céad Bliana i Roinn na Gaeilge, i gColáiste na Ollscoile, Gaillimh. Tá Tina ina cónaí i mBaile Uí Mhornáin i gContae na Mí agus ag obair mar mhúinteoir i gColáiste Íosagáin i mBaile an Bhothair, Baile Atha Cliath. Is í Tina an iníon is óige leis an scríbhneoir Siobhán Ní Shúilleabhán.

Sandra Bunting

DOWN FROM THE HILLS

Until you see it devour a kitten,
you imagine it just another dog.
Go ahead and open the door:
you won't be able to get out,
alpha-wolf blocking the way
grey eyes wary, scraggy hair on end.

Night falls,
full moon against black sky,
the howling begins,
no stop, no let up,
no hiding place
from a fear we had forgotten,
and you wonder what made
it choose your door.

Deep down you know
and that knowledge
chills you to the bone.
He is the last wolf
desperate to find a mate
before a hunter claims
his bounty of blood.

PLAYING HOUSE

My mother, when at college,
spent the summer with her parents
at their cottage by the sea
and discovered, hidden by spruce,
an abandoned shed behind the summer home
on which she spent her holiday fixing up
until it was clean, furnished and cosy
and when she left for studies in the city,
she told herself it would always be there:
still playing house after all the years.

After a winter filled with summer plans,
she ran without stopping to her place:
the door wouldn't open hard as she pulled.
Tried the windows, the door at the back
but there was no way in.
'Why is that old shed closed up?'
Now that it had worth, a gift to her brother,
living far away, so he'd come home.
Before it belonged to no one.
Now it had a lock and key, and was not hers.

Growing up with the story, I made nests
in closets, in attics, in a clump of trees.
I slept in doorways of big houses,
went off without a word to Latin America,
and tried settling in France and in Spain.
I got my own house with a husband,
two daughters, a dog and a cat,
looked out through windows splashed with rain
as I painted each room in my colours.
But at the word home, I would go back
to that shed in the wood I never lived in.

A random photograph showed up your face
amongst the tumult of the wild river Corrib.

Lost in rough current under Wolfe Tone Bridge,
you couldn't be seen with the naked eye.

It was as if we needed the camera as a medium
to join the different worlds of ours and yours.

There you were on photographic paper,
grey-green calm, drowned daughter of chieftains.

Are you saying that it is better to die for love
and bathe in the soothing balm of water,

or is that your song heard in the screeching wind
as you float, forever condemned, beneath our feet?

Sandra Bunting is a member of the Galway Writers'
Workshop and is on the editorial board of the Galway literary
magazine *Crannóg*. She was brought up in Canada, went to
secondary school in Dublin, studied Communications and
went on to complete a Masters in Writing at NUI Galway. She
has had work published in Ireland, England and Canada and
her first collection of poetry will be published soon.

Mary Mannion

LOVE

The spinster lady came in and shook the rain from her hair, face and body and nobody saw her tender neck or her delicate hands. She stood by the electric fire and the smell of rain reminded her of long ago when once she had said to her mother: 'I'd love to go out and run in the rain with a bar of soap and to wash and have bubbles all over me', and her mother had said 'Such talk is sinful'. Everything was sinful to her mother, even talk itself. Now she was silenced for ever and the spinster lady could stay out all night if she liked, but it was too late now because she had no interest in anything other than in being sensible. And once she had despised such a thing.

She made herself some tea and boiled an egg and then from force of habit she washed up because mother said there's nothing worse than dirty cups left gathering dust. Then she looked out at the night. The avenue was quiet and bare trees stood nakedly leaning out to her and she loved them as she always had. She hated cluttered up dressings on trees and on people. I am the original streaker, she told herself, and she smiled.

The spinster lady was in a strange mood that night. The smell of the rain and the stark trees had brought back sensations she had forgotten ever existed. She was eighteen years old again and she wanted not to go to bed, not to put in rollers and not to put out the light and get a good night's sleep. She wanted excitement, but spinster ladies of fifty-one years didn't get much excitement. There are barriers preventing spinster ladies from entering places of entertainment. The young can congregate in warm lounge bars and comfortable couples of eighty-two years can be smiled on in such places and bachelors gay of one-hundred-and-eight can be one of the boys but spinster ladies of fifty-one years are unacceptable. 'To hell with it', said the spinster lady, 'I'm going out'. So she pinned up her hair with all the hair pins and then she pulled them out and let the grey and brown soft stripes envelop her neck and shoulders and she went out into the night. As the bus took her into town she thought of how much a creature of habit she had become. It was now ten past ten and unthinkable that Miss Cleary should be riding on an omnibus to the city, bent on pleasure. On pleasure, on brandy, on a happy evening, sang her heart. You have the change of life over you, said her reason, you're a typical old maid now, you're finished. I've never been there so I've never changed, sang her heart, and tonight I'm on my way.

She walked bravely up the stairs of the Golden Goblet and made her way to the counter.

'A double brandy, please', said Miss Cleary in a very loud voice.

Soon she was wrapped in a haze of warmth and she never noticed the nudges of the couples or the sniggers of the bright young things nor even the crude remarks of the bachelors.

Down the stairs tumbled Miss Cleary and three people - one a retired civil servant, one a Miss Marilyn McDonald and one a fellow of the student type - saw her warm pink drawers, seconds at a reduced rate, and on that Friday evening a very private person rolled into the gutter and a crowd gathered and discussed her.

Miss Cleary was vaguely aware of many voices. She did not know that it was the young man of the student type who had put her into a taxi and given the driver his last few pounds. She never knew a thing about the journey home but here she was inside her own door and she was still very drunk.

She made her way to the bathroom and pulled neat towels from the rail and flung the red face-cloth - mother's - up to the ceiling and eventually came into contact with a fat yellow bar of soap. Pulling off her clothes she ran like a mad person out into the rain. The rain poured down and soap bubbles ran into gutters and Miss Cleary tightly wrapped her thin arms round a poor thin brown tree and sang to it. This is the song she sang.

'Are you lonely, my little baby? Mammy has come to mind you. I'm sorry I left you for a while. Your father was a vulgar man, he went away and left me all alone and I had to give you up. I know the orphanage was bleak and awful and I know you missed your mammy but I'm here now. I'll give you shelter and protection from all of them. From all of them with their families and their engagement rings and their cheap jokes. Mammy will comb your dear brown hair, and did you eat your porridge today love, and if you didn't sure it doesn't matter. Your own Mammy will smile and let her little girl have cornflakes even if it is winter time. I have a treat for you my love. Mammy and you will go to the Estoria after school this evening. We'll leave the dirty dishes and your Mammy will buy you sweets and we'll sit at the pictures like two friends and we'll laugh in the dark at the lovers on the screen and the lovers in the audience, because your Mammy doesn't think such things are dirty, and doesn't think you should be protected from seeing love, because your Mammy loves her little girl, and we will wait for the film two times if you wish, and millions of other treats I have for my little darling'.

And the rain poured down. Miss Cleary's private body was exposed to wind and cold and felt nothing. She sang to the tree of how her baby could bring in her friends in the evening and how, when she was old enough, she could mix with boys and have parties and she sang of all the things her mother had told her were bad and she told her baby she was pretty, and that she was going to have great times, and she never mentioned sin and she never ever told her about the things all men are out for.

Miss Cleary was thin and Miss Cleary was greying and Miss Cleary was typical of the typical spinster lady but tonight she was a fat warm Mamma in a flowery apron, baking cakes for her daughter's twenty first birthday party, and tonight she was someone to run to and tonight she was more motherly than all of the mothers in all of the houses on all of that avenue.

Paddy Grogan, the night worker, saw her at seven ten a.m. He was shocked. His first thought was to protect the innocent. He wrapped his coat round her and then telephoned Dr Ward.

'Of course, when the doc saw her condition he knew she'd had it', he told the lads in the local on Sunday morning.

There were many who gave opinions on what caused such a thing to happen. Frustration was the agreed common factor. On Sunday afternoon when the children were out of the room, fifty men told fifty wives about Miss Cleary stark naked hanging onto a tree.

'Where did they take her?' asked Mrs O'Rourke.

'The asylum according to Grogan', said her husband.

'Those are always the type', said his wife, 'I wish she had my problems and someone to worry about except herself. I'd like to see that one having a couple of kids. Too damn selfish, that's her problem. A typical old maid. Thank God none of the kids saw her'.

'And her mother was such a lady', said Mrs O'Dea.

And the smug became smugger and they congratulated each other at the shops on Monday morning. In fifty places of employment fifty men told an average of ten co-workers and soon the whole north side had the story.

Miss Cleary developed pneumonia and it seemed she might not survive, but she did after all. She is still being treated for her nerves and the doctors are unanimous that it's a distinct case of sexual frustration. The fact of the soap points to religious scruples and the contact with the tree is inhibited sex and, if she ever leaves the hospital, she will be well provided for with valium and librium and all other kinds of items that are manufactured to help misfits to stay within the law and, above all, so that innocent children may be protected.

The young man of the student type sometimes wonders whatever happened the gentle-faced woman with the shy smile and the warm pink drawers, seconds at a reduced rate.

Mary Mannion is a native of Lower Salthill. She worked as a legal secretary until 2002. At present she is a teacher's assistant in a primary school in Dublin. She published a number of stories in the New Irish Writing page in the *Irish Press* and also a one-act play, *The Write Stuff*, which was performed in Andrew's Lane Theatre. She is now working on a novel.

Margaret Boner

THE DUBLIN TRAIN

First hour gone by
Newspapers discarded.
The woman along the aisle sighs
Looking across the hard landscape
'It's a cauld oul Saharda'

Cows huddle together
On a mud cratered hill
Sheep and white capped rocks
Keep company.

Solid grey stone station-houses
Lie abandoned, windows blocked.
Black clouds closing over a low sky.
Chilling.

Leaving Tullamore
The sky is splashed pink
A glowing January twilight
Brings sharp brilliance
To bare twigs silhouetted in its light.

Moving through the darkening countryside
Distant lights pierce the land.
'Our last scheduled stop before Dublin'
I'm reminded of other journeys long ago:

Portarlington to Dublin
Would we ever be there?
The excitement of
The zoo, the Panto, the lights!

Later still,
Friends working in Dublin
Living in flats
Hair appointments
Coffee in Switzers
Rugby club hops
Mac Liammóir at the Gaiety.
The importance of it all.

This time
A new century
Forty years on.
Portarlington to Dublin
I still travel with childlike delight
Middle-aged,
Remembering.

UNTITLED

This is a wet warm January day
Full of buds and new beginnings.
The mood is for bringing me back.

Christmas eve snow
Recorded by M
To be seen and marvelled at
Until the next white Christmas!

St. Stephen's Day at Menlo pier
Two boats submerged, frozen.
Swans watching languorously
Moving inevitably towards me.

Rapid disturbance as
Wings clash with ice
To no avail
They turn and sail away.

A small bird
(Unhindered by such restrictions)
Marches towards me on the ice
Slipping, straightening
And coming apace.
Pecking at morsels invisible to me
Fooled by images under the ice?

Muddy reeds magiced into crimson
By the low bright sun
Enveloping the swans.
And all the time
Birds flying over and back,
Playing games,
Are they guarding what is below?

Dramatically the colours change.
Freezing fog unfurls in slow motion
Reaching into every crevice of the scene.
Screeching gulls fly in
To land awkwardly on the ice.

Unnoticed, the swans are gone.
A feeling of unease hurries me away
As though it were wrong to be
In this place for now.

Margaret Nicholson Boner was born in Galway and educated at Scoil Fhursa, Taylor's Hill and UCG. She holds a BA from UCG, where she worked as an administrative assistant. Having reared her family, she returned to UCG and worked in the Nursing Library until her recent retirement. She is married to John Boner and has one daughter and four sons. While her family were young, she wrote a story for them which is still in a drawer! More recently she has been writing poetry and attending writing workshops.

Mary Dempsey

ENJOYING MY MOTHER

Look at her carefully, a blue foulard tied around her head. It has a satin quality with a weave of white flowers. She is wearing a mauve trouser suit and sits in the sun reading a book on astronomy. What is she preparing for? A trip through the night sky when her daughters have vanished? Olive and her son James are also there for tea. We sit outside the basement floor, cursing the wind for interrupting the sun. Rather Olive and my mother are cursing the wind. I am sitting in the windbreak of my mother's bulk, reading a teenage story by Collette, called 'Ripening Seed'. My mother eyes it a little suspiciously.

My mother's reading keeps her out of harms way, she can be present and enjoy the company. A little deaf, tricky moments fly over her head. This is compensation for too much child-bearing, age brings its rewards and precious silences.

My sister Sarah rings up. She'd like to come over but feels that two sisters at a time are plenty and makes do with cooking for herself. Ann rings from Tullamore, her son has come third in the All Ireland Athletics. We respond with oohs and aahs. We regret not being there to see Luca perform.

A family spread out as far as Canada. If I had been a son, would it have been different? I mucked out horses' stables and rounded up sheep. I hated being indoors.

Now I am a stranger who arrives in a green car, bearing strawberries and apple pie, caught in the elastic web of family. Or am I attached to rope, thinking I've travelled far?

There is a pink geranium on the windowsill of my apartment, a blue pot beside it with a painted boat and white sail. Who is pulling now, what place in my heart is being tinkered with? Am I staying or going?

I belong to this pink geranium that insists on blooming. There is no end or beginning, only the middle years that keep floating.

LILY

An excerpt from a poetic monologue

I don't know how my mother managed

Ritual is the key
keeps away the horrors

Up early out the door
hello to the porter
a quick chat with the *boulanger*
Parisians in slippers
stroll through the inevitable pigeons
click the code in through the main door

Things went from bad to worse
the teapot came to grief
then the lampshade
cups that had been in the place for years

There is comfort in arguments
the tenacious grip on something crumbling
things that get said
the door banging
locking him out
then making up

The same thing happening somewhere else

Things came to a crunch

I'm quieter now

I do the circle over the rope bridge
down by the artificial lake
and the battered trees
listening to my French tapes
mouthing a foreign accent
a jumped-up Artaud

I like the silence
no traffic around here
just stone steps
a hundred steps to climb if
you want to see me

I often see my grandfather
as I go down
his white hair
his mouth wide open

He's telling me something

Do you remember that time Lily
when you were no higher
than the wheel of my bicycle
I was so proud of you
walking beside me

Your little hand reaching up
to hold the crossbar
down the *bóithrín*
still unsteady on your legs
your smile and baby chatter

Grandad I remember you yawning
your lower teeth were brown
your mouth as big as an aquarium

A fish out of water

I had a dream once
your head was floating underwater
your beautiful white hair streaming
towards the bottom of the ocean
I was in a small gold boat
trying to fish you out

Mary Dempsey is a writer, photographer and filmmaker from Galway. She has given readings in Ireland and abroad and was invited by Galway City Library to give readings in Parma, Italy (2000) and Brittany (2001) under the Socrates Programme for Adult Education. She wrote and performed a dramatic monologue, entitled, *Lily*, for The Contemporary Irish Women Writers' Conference, NUI, Dublin (1999) and has been short listed for a number of poetry prizes. She has made four short films which have been shown at festivals in Ireland and abroad and broadcast on RTÉ and TG4. She is the recipient of an Irish Arts Council bursary and received project awards from the Galway Film Centre and Filmbase.

My Miracle

The Pope is responsible.

Cynical as I was about the Pontiff's visit to Ireland, when the Papal helicopter circled over Galway's racecourse, almost against my will, I turned on the television. To my amazement, as John Paul knelt to kiss the ground, I too knelt, and when he said: 'People of Ireland, I lof you', joy, excitement, sadness, filled me. I found myself humming hymns I hadn't sung since childhood, and, as I joined in the singing of 'Totus Tuus', tears filled my eyes. In the Pope's honour, school was closed. But no matter how I tried, I couldn't concentrate on correcting mid-term tests. I was glad when Felicity 'phoned inviting me to join her and two American visitors for dinner.

I first made friends with Felicity - a small bubbly, blue eyed, blonde, with a well-rounded cuddly body - whilst I was working in London some years ago. Later, when, due to her excessive charity towards an elderly male client, Felicity was fired from her job as a social worker in Camden Town, she decided to see what Galway had to offer. Fond as I was of my friend, I tried to discourage her from seeking work here. I explained Ireland's sexual taboos and inhibitions and the Irish male's interest in drink, rather than in, to use her own terminology, 'the magic of sex'.

She still wanted to come.

'Don't worry', she laughed. 'I'll manage even if I have to import a bag full of aphrodisiacs'.

She never needed them. Whereas I, who am six foot tall, dark, sallow-faced and angular, with a rather unfortunate nose, and, they tell me, a severe expression, could well have done with some. In my thirty one years, I have only had three lovers. All unsatisfactory.

Number I, if you will excuse my frankness, had a habit of picking his nose after we had sex.

Number II, immediately we'd finished, would dash to the wash basin to place his manhood under the cold tap. Watching him through half-closed eyes, my shy nature prevented me asking if this were an act of hygiene or of penance.

Number III, the poorest performer, would hum 'Veni Creator Spiritus' throughout the act. In moments of climax, his humming became an exultant cry. Not even neighbours banging on the bedroom wall could silence his crescendo.

My three lovers had left me with a fear that I might be frigid. But since Felicity began giving me vivid accounts of her sexual activities, which she calls 'adventures', I have gained enormous pleasure from what magazine articles and the television show 'Real Personal', call 'vicarious sex'. Sometimes, in fact, I find myself trembling with excitement, as I soak in detailed descriptions of Felicity's sex life. Felicity says that, deep in my sub-conscious, some spring needs to be released if I am ever to enjoy the wonders of direct sex. She believes that those reared in Ireland's peculiar brand of Catholicism, need to be reprogrammed if they are to learn that 'It is in giving we receive'.

But to return to the night of the Pope's visit, when Felicity opened her door, I asked if she'd seen John Paul on television. Rolling her eyes, she said that she had, adding that he was pure gorgeous and that his sexy voice made her melt. 'Men make me melt', is one of Felicity's frequent sayings. And, each time I hear her say it, I feel that I should love, if only once, to experience this melting feeling, which, she swears, must surpass ecstasy.

As soon as we were sitting down sipping wine, she began to fill me in on the previous night's 'adventure'. A

Government Minister, whom I obviously can't name, but one whom I would have thought of as rather a cold fish, had performed in a most imaginative and exciting way on her sheepskin rug. Stretching out on the rug, eyes closed, she relived the experience. I was furious when the ringing of the doorbell interrupted my friend's flow of words and my mounting pleasure.

'How's it going, chum?'

She hugged her guests. One was quite attractive in a clean-cut American way. The other, who alternately chewed tobacco and cleaned his teeth with a matchstick, was my idea of a lumberjack.

By the end of the meal, I was bored. Both men talked loudly and in jargon I could barely understand. After dinner, Felicity disappeared with Jules into the garden leaving me to listen to bleary-eyed, tobacco-chewing Chuck, rabbiting on about his dart-playing wife.

'Yes', his voice was proud, 'my Meryl is one of the best woman dart players in Arkansas'.

When Felicity and Jules returned, under pretext of helping with coffee, I joined her in the kitchen to whisper that I must be off.

'Will you', she asked, 'be a honey and keep Chuck company for awhile?'

When I told her I'd have to leave immediately after coffee, she shrugged and I followed her into the living room where she turned on the television to watch the Pope bless a group at Knock airport.

Something happened.

I removed my eyes from the Pope, fixed them on Chuck and became filled with a melting feeling. Tears blurred my vision. I accepted when Chuck suggested that he walk the short distance home with me. Tenderly, we held hands. And when he asked if he could come in, I answered, 'But of course'. I was surprised and delighted by his love-making.

'Wonderful. Much better', a voice, which had to be my own, answered as, haltingly, he asked if the second time was better than the first. 'It is in giving that we receive', echoed and re-echoed in my head.

Afterwards, I stroked his callused hands and interjected encouraging comments as I listened to more dart-playing wife stories. We made love again on the floor. I kissed him a lingering goodbye.

Awake next day, I was miserable and totally confused. The all-embracing spirit of Felicity had briefly entered me, only to disappear with the dawn of a new day. When I'd flung sheets and duvet cover into the washing machine, I showered and showered.

In the evening, I again turned on the T.V. to watch an exhausted Pope leave Ireland. Listening to 'People of Ireland, I lof you', I wanted Chuck back. I would be so tender to him. A sensation. Yes. A melting sensation filled me as gently I rocked my body to and fro.

Margaret Faherty has published short stories in many literary journals and magazines; she was an award winner for both short fiction and poetry at the Moore Literary Convention. Her work has featured on BBC Radio 4 and on RTÉ's Sunday Miscellany and the Living Word. She has completed two novels.

Trish Casey

IN HONOUR OF ANN
(desecrated woman-child)

She takes the bus to Wicklow to visit The Hag;
willingly enters the domain of the damned;
sips tea from a cracked cup, smokes cigarettes,
listening to the walls lament.

She downs a few at the local,
stands The Hag a jar,
smokes more cigarettes,
tells The Hag she's tired and takes her leave;
sinks through the shroud of that demented hush, alone;
knocks back some of The Hag's Valium,
creeps to her childhood bed,
pulls the covers over her head, and waits,
waits for the hammering;
the shouting and the hammering on the front door,
'Y'bitch, y'two faced whore, let me in! Y'trollop, let me in!'

She listens, savouring every sound
and laughs and laughs
the simple, sublime giggle
of *The Goodie*.
Then she sleeps.

SAFFRON AND SUCCESS
The Interview

Saffron Risingstone was born the President
of a multinational computer software corporation.
A multimillionaire fluent in fifteen languages,
she spent the first ten years of her life asking,
'Why me? Why wasn't I born normal?'

Now aged twenty, having endured since birth
the frustration of realised aspirations
and fulfilled expectations,
she has learned to live with such challenges.
Reclining opposite me
in a daring tangerine Versace number,
she grimaces, 'Okay, I'm perfect,
but I'm alone in my perfection. *That* isn't easy'.
Pursing her painted lips,
she takes a second sip of her Martini - dry.

Indeed, Saffron Risingstone is perfect;
a svelte five feet eleven inches,
her teeth an orthodontist's dream,
her sallow complexion flawless and radiant.
Under the light of a Mediterranean sunset,
she fixes her mesmerising eyes earnestly upon me.

'Sometimes I still ask "why?"' she murmurs,
as she draws her slender manicured fingers
through her blonde flowing tresses.
'Why did I have to be born perfect,
into the most idyllic of material worlds?
But mostly I've resigned myself,
and I live with the social privilege,
the opulent lifestyle, the enviable success
and the drop-dead-gorgeous looks as best I can'.

Yes, despite everything,
Saffron Risingstone remains hopeful.
She leans forward confidingly,
'I sometimes glimpse another me,
the ordinary person, that perhaps, I could be ...'
She gazes at something I cannot see,
with an unconscious shrug of those fine bone shoulders,
a wistful hint in those bewitching green eyes,
a strain of melancholy
caressing that fulsome magenta mouth.

THE TOOLS OF THE MASTER

She fucks till four,
and when he sleeps
she slips her foreign-holiday-body
with that super-turbo-top-up-tan
into her tailored suit
and Italian shoes.

Zips back to her apartment to sleep a few hours -
power showers, pops some Prozac,
scans her personal organiser,
checks her voice mail, grips her briefcase
and clicks her way to her customised convertible
in the Residents Only car park.

She cuts, at eight, into the rush hour traffic -
taps her manicured Crimson Flame fingernails
against the leather-clad steering wheel
and mouths to the latest *hothothot* radio tune:

Ooh, baby baby, I'm so free.
Ooh, baby baby, you'll never own me.
Ooohhh, baby ...

HMM?

She lies on a bed in a cubicle in Casualty,
a nurse checking her pulse.
'Susan ...
Joyce, isn't it?'
'Yeah'.
'So Susan,
what possessed you to try this then,
hmm?'

Susan assumes that's a rhetorical question.
Nurse ...
Stanton
hardly cares to hear the hackneyed tale
of an alcoholic rapist
for a father
and a near catatonic heap
for a mother.
Nurse Stanton is hardly interested
in the details
of a trip to England for an abortion.
She hardly wants to know
the specifics
of a previous hospitalisation
for an eating disorder.
Nurse Stanton hardly cares to hear the truth at all,
does she now,
hmm?

'Well ...
I wanted to go away for the weekend
but I had no money,
so I decided to take an overdose instead'.

'I'd advise you not to be so smart, missy.
We'll have to pump you out.
It's a nasty procedure.
Do you want me to contact anyone for you?'

A doctor emerges, clipboard in hand,
from behind the drawn curtain.
'Susan ...
Joyce, isn't it?
So Susan,
what was the purpose of all this then,
hmm?'
'Dr J. ...
Kingston, isn't it?
So, Dr Kingston,
take a flying fuck, why don't you,
hmm?'

Trish Casey, from the harbour town of Cobh in Co. Cork, is a graduate of the Gaiety School of Acting. She won the performance prize at the RTÉ Rattlebag Slam in 2003. Last year she won the Cúirt Festival Grand Slam. Her prize was a trip to Chicago to perform at the Green Mill Tavern (the home of slam) and Chicago Cultural Centre. She has since been invited to perform at the University of North Florida in the coming autumn. Over the last year Trish's work has appeared in the *Irish Times* and the national heritage magazine *Heritage Outlook*. She is soon to be published in a new Leaving Cert geography textbook. Trish has performed her work at numerous venues throughout Galway City and county, as well as in Dublin, Limerick, Cork, Manchester and Swansea. She currently lives in Galway.

Dís

' 'Sheáin?'

'Hu?'

'Cuir síos an páipéar agus bí ag caint liom'.

'Á anois, muna bhféadfaidh fear suí cois tine agus páipéar a léamh tar éis a lá oibre'.

'Bhíos-sa ag obair leis feadh an lae, sa tigh'.

'Hu?'

'Ó, tá go maith, trom blúire den bpáipéar agus ná habair, "geobhair é go léir tar éis tamaill"'.

'Ní rabhas chun é sin a rá. Seo duit'.

Lánúin cois tine tráthnóna.

Leanbh ina chodladh sa phram.

Stéig feola ag díreo sa chistin.

Carr ag díluacháil sa gharáiste.

Méadar leictreach ag cuntas chuige a chuid aonad ...

'Hé! Táim anso! 'Sheáin! Táim anso!'

'Hu?'

'Táim sa pháipéar'.

'Tusa? Cén áit? N'fhacas-sa tú'.

'Agus tá tusa ann leis'.

'Cad tá ort? Léas-sa an leathanach san roimh é thabhairt duit'.

'Tá's agam. Deineann tú i gcónaí. Ach chuaigh an méid sin i ngan fhios duit. Táimid araon anso. Mar gheall orainne atá sé'.

'Cad a bheadh mar gheall orainne ann? Ní dúrtsa faic le héinne'.

'Ach dúrtsa. Cuid mhaith'.

'Cé leis? Cad é? Taispeáin dom! Cad air go bhfuil tú ag caint?'

'Féach ansan. Toradh suirbhé a deineadh. Deirtear ann go bhfuil an ceathrú cuid de mhná pósta na tíre míshona, míshásta. Táimse ansan, ina measc'.

'Tusa? Míshona, míshásta? Sin é an chéad chuid a chuala de'.

'Tá sé ansan anois os comhair do dhá shúl. Mise duine des na mná a bhí sa tsuirbhé sin. Is cuimhin liom an mhaidean go maith. I mí Eanáir ab ea é; drochaimsir, doircheacht, dochmacht, billí, *sales* ar siúl agus gan aon airgead chucu, an sórt san. Eanáir, Feabhra, Márta, Aibreán, Bealtaine, Meitheamh. 'Cheart go mbeadh sé aici aon lá anois'.

'Cad a bheadh aici?'

'Leanbh. Cad eile bheadh ag bean ach leanbh!'

'Cén bhean?'

'An bhean a tháinig chugam an mhaidean san'.

'Cad chuige, in ainm Dé?'

'Chun an suirbhé a dhéanamh, agus ísligh do ghlór nó dúiseoir an leanbh. Munar féidir le lánú suí síos le chéile tráthnóna agus labhairt go deas ciúin sibhialta le chéile'.

'Ní raibh uaim ach an páipéar a léamh'.

'Sin é é. Is tábhachtaí an páipéar ná mise. Is tábhachtaí an rud atá le léamh sa pháipéar ná an rud atá le rá agamsa. Bhuel, mar sin, seo leat agus léigh é. An rud atá le rá agam, tá sé sa pháipéar sa tsuirbhé. Ag an saol go léir le léamh. Sin mise feasta. Staitistic. Sin é a chuirfidh mé síos leis in aon fhoirm eile bheidh le líonadh agam. *Occupation? Statistic.* Níos deise ná *housewife*, cad a déarfá?'

'Hu?'

'Is cuma leat cé acu chomh fada is dheinim obair *housewife*. Sin é dúrtsa léi leis'.

'Cad dúraís léi?'

'Ná tugtar fé ndeara aon ní a dheineann tú mar bhean tí, ach nuair ná deineann tú é. Cé thugann fé ndeara go bhfuil an t-urlár glan? Ach má bhíonn sé salach, sin rud eile'.

'Cad eile a dúraís léi?'

'Chuile rud'.

'Fúmsa leis?'

'Fúinn araon, a thaisce. Ná cuireadh sé isteach ort. Ní bhíonn aon ainmneacha leis an tsuirbhé - chuile rud neamhphearsanta, coimeádtar chuile eolas go discréideach fé rún. Compútar a dheineann amach an toradh ar deireadh, a dúirt sí. Ní cheapas riamh go mbeinn im lón compútair!'

'Stróinséir mná a shiúlann isteach 'on tigh chugat, agus tugann tú gach eolas di fúinne?'

'Ach bhí jab le déanamh aici. N'fhéadfainn gan cabhrú léi. An rud bocht, tá sí pósta le dhá bhliain, agus 'bhreá léi leanbh, ach an t-árasán atá acu ní lomhálfaidh an t-úinéir aon leanbh ann agus táid araon ag obair chun airgead tí a sholáthar mar anois tá leanbh chucu agus caithfidh siad a bheith amuigh as an árasán, agus níor mhaith leat go gcaillfeadh sí a post, ar mhaith? N'fhéadfainn an doras a dhúnadh sa phus uirthi, maidean fhuar fhliuch mar é, an bhféadfainn?'

'Ach níl aon cheart ag éinne eolas príobháideach mar sin fháil'.

'Ní di féin a bhí sí á lorg. Bhí sraith ceisteanna tugtha di le cur agus na freagraí le scrí síos. Jab a bhí ann di sin. Jab maith leis, an áirithe sin sa ló, agus costaisí taistil. Beidh mé ábalta an sorn nua san a cheannach as'.

'Tusa? Conas?'

'Bog réidh anois. Ní chuirfidh sé isteach ar an gcáin ioncaim agatsa. Lomhálann siad an áirithe sin; *working wife's allowance* mar thugann siad air - amhail is nach aon *working wife* tú aige baile, ach is cuma san'.

'Tá tusa chun oibriú lasmuigh? Cathain, munar mhiste dom a fhiafraí?'

'Níl ann ach obair shealadach, ionadaíocht a dhéanamh di faid a bheidh sí san ospidéal chun an leanbh a bheith aici, agus ina dhiaidh san. Geibheann siad ráithe saoire don leanbh'.

'Agus cad mar gheall ar do leanbhsa?'

'Tabharfaidh mé liom é sa bhascaed i gcúl an chairr, nó má bhíonn sé dúisithe, im bhaclainn. Cabhair a bheidh ann dom. Is maith a thuigeann na tincéirí san'.

'Cad é? Cén bhaint atá ag tincéirí leis an gcúram?'

'Ní dhúnann daoine doras ar thincéir mná go mbíonn leanbh ina baclainn'.

'Tuigim. Tá tú ag tógaint an jab seo, ag dul ag tincéireacht ó dhoras go doras'.

'Ag suirbhéireacht ó dhoras go doras'.

'Mar go bhfuil tú míshona, míshásta sa tigh'.

'Cé dúirt é sin leat?'

'Tusa'.

'Go rabhas míshona, míshásta. Ní dúrt riamh'.

'Dúraís. Sa tsuirbhé. Féach an toradh ansan sa pháipéar'.

'Á, sa tsuirbhé! Ach sin scéal eile. Ní gá gurb í an fhírinne a inseann tú sa tsuirbhé'.

'Cad deireann tú?'

'Dá bhfeicfeá an liosta ceisteanna, fé rudaí chomh príobháideach! Stróinséir mná a shiúlann isteach, go dtabharfainnse fios gach aon ní di, meas óinsí atá agat orm, ab ea? D'fhreagraíos a cuid ceisteanna, a dúrt leat, sin rud eile ar fad'.

'Ó!'

'Agus maidir leis an jab, táim á thógaint chun airgead soirn nua a thuilleamh, sin uile. Ar aon tslí, tusa fé ndear é'.

'Cad é? Mise fé ndear cad é?'

'Na rudaí a dúrt léi'.

'Mise? Bhíos-sa ag obair'.

'Ó, bhís! Nuair a bhí an díobháil déanta'.

'Cén díobháil?'

'Ní cuimhin liom anois cad a dheinis, ach dheinis rud éigin an mhaidean san a chuir an gomh orm, nó b'fhéidir gurb é an oíche roimh ré féin é, n'fheadar. Agus bhí an mhaidean chomh gruama, agus an tigh chomh tóin-thar-ceann tar éis an deireadh seachtaine, agus an bille ESB tar éis teacht, nuair a bhuail sí chugam isteach lena liosta ceisteanna, cheapas gur anuas ós na Flaithis a tháinig sí chugam. Ó, an sásamh a fuaireas scaoileadh liom féin agus é thabhairt ó thalamh d'fhearaibh. Ó, an t-ualach a thóg sé dem chroí! Diabhail chruthanta a bhí iontu, dúrt, gach aon diabhal duine acu, bhíomar marbh riamh acu, dúrt, inár sclábhaithe bhíomar acu, dúrt. Cad ná dúrt! Na scéalta a chumas di! Níor cheapas riamh go raibh féith na cumadóireachta ionam'.

'Agus chreid sí go rabhais ag insint na fírinne, go rabhais ag tabhairt freagra macánta ar gach aon cheist a chuir sí?'

'Bhuel, ní raibh aon *lie detector* aici, is dóigh liom. N'fhaca é ar aon tslí. Ní déarfainn gurb é a cúram é, ní mhór dóibh síceolaí a bheith acu i mbun an jaib mar sin. Ó, chuir sí an cheist agus thugas-sa an freagra, agus sin a raibh air. Agus bhí cupa caife againn ansin, agus bhíomar araon lántsásta'.

'Ach ná feiceann tú ná fuil san ceart? Mná eile ag léamh torthaí mar seo. Ceathrú de mhná pósta na tíre míshásta? Cothóidh sé míshástacht iontusan leis'.

'Níl aon leigheas agamsa ar conas a chuireann siad rudaí sna páipéir. D'fhéadfaidís a rá go raibh trí ceathrúna de mhná na tíre sásta sona, ná féadfaidís, ach féach a ndúradar? Ach sé a gcúramsan an páipéar a dhíol, agus ní haon nath le héinne an té atá sona, sásta. Sé an té atá míshásta, ag déanamh agóide, a gheibheann éisteacht sa tsaol so, ó chuile mheán cumarsáide. Sin mar atá; ní mise a chum ná a cheap. Aon ní amháin a cheapas féin a bhí bunoscionn leis an tsuirbhé, ná raibh a dóthain ceisteanna aici. Chuirfinnse a thuilleadh leo. Ní hamháin 'an bhfuil tú sásta, ach an dóigh leat go mbeidh tú sásta, má mhaireann tú leis?'

'Conas?'

'Na Sínigh fadó, bhí an ceart acu, tá's agat'.

'Conas?'

'Sa nós san a bhí acu, nuair a cailltí an fear, a bhean chéile a dhó ina theannta. Bhí ciall leis'.

'Na hIndiaigh a dheineadh san, narbh ea?'

'Cuma cé acu, bhí ciall leis mar nós. Bhuel, cad eile atá le déanamh léi? Tá gá le bean chun leanaí a chur ar an saol agus iad a thógaint, agus nuair a bhíd tógtha agus bailithe leo, tá gá léi fós chun bheith ag tindeáil ar an bhfear. Chuige sin a phós sé í, nach ea? Ach nuair a imíonn seisean, cad ar a mairfidh sí ansan? *Redundant!* Tar éis a saoil. Ach ní fhaghann sí aon *redundancy money*, ach pinsean beag suarach baintrí'.

'Ach cad a mheasann tú is ceart a dhéanamh?'

'Níl a fhios agam. Sa tseansaol, cuirtí i gcathaoir súgáin sa chúinne í ag riar seanchaíochta agus seanleigheasanna, má bhí sí mór leis an mbean mhic, nó ag bruíon is ag achrann léi muna raibh, ach bhí a háit aici sa chomhluadar. Anois, níl faic aici. Sa tslí ar gach éinne atá sí. Bhí ciall ag na Sínigh. Meas tú an mbeadh fáil in aon áit ar an leabhar dearg san?'

'Cén leabhar dearg?'

'Le Mao? 'Dheas liom é léamh. 'Dheas liom rud éigin a bheith le léamh agam nuair ná geibhim an páipéar le léamh, agus nuair ná fuil éinne agam a labhródh liom. Ach beidh mo jab agam sara fada. Eanáir, Feabhra, Márta, Aibreán, Bealtaine, Meitheamh; tá sé in am. Tá sé thar am. Dúirt sí go mbeadh sí i dteagbháil liom mí roimh ré. Ní théann aon leanbh thar dheich mí agus a dhícheall a dhéanamh ... Is é sin má bhí leanbh i gceist riamh ná árasán ach oiread. B'fhéidir ná raibh sí pósta féin. B'fhéidir gur ag insint éithigh dom a bhí sí chun go mbeadh trua agam di, agus go bhfreagróinn a cuid ceisteanna. Agus chaitheas mo mhaidean léi agus bhí oiread le déanamh agam an mhaidean chéanna; níochán is gach aon ní, ach shuíos síos ag freagairt ceisteanna di agus ag tabhairt caife di, agus gan aon fhocal den bhfírinne ag teacht as a béal! Bhuel, cuimhnigh air sin! Nach mór an lúbaireacht a bhíonn i ndaoine!'

Lánúin cois tine tráthnóna.

An leanbh ina chodladh sa phram.

An fear ina chodladh fén bpáipéar.

An stéig feola ag díreo sa chistin.

An carr ag díluacháil sa gharáiste.

An bhean

Prioc preac

liom leat

ann as.

Tic toc an mhéadair leictrigh ag cuntas chuige na n-aonad.

As cheantar Bhaile an Fhirtéaraigh i gCorca Dhuibhne an scríbhneoir **Siobhán Ní Shúilleabhán**. Fuair sí oiliúint mar bhunmhúinteoir agus bhí sí ag múineadh i mBaileÁtha Cliath ar feadh ceithre bliana. Chaith sí trí bliana ag obair ar Fhoclóir Thomás de Bhálraithe. Tá cúig úrscéal, ocht leabhar do dhaoine óga, dráma, cnuasach gearrscéal agus cnuasach dánta foilsithe aici. Tá trí dráma léi léirithe ar theilifís, naoi gcinn ar raidió agus dosaen ar an stáitse. Bronnadh an *Irish Life Award* uirthi i 1974, Duais na Mílaoise Chló Iarchonnacht d'Urscéal, duaiseanna difriúla i gComórtais Liteartha an Oireachtais agus duaiseanna éagsúla i Seachtain na Scríbhneoirí Lios Tuathail. Tá Siobhán pósta le Pádraig Mac Enrí agus tá siad ina gcónaí i gCathair na Gaillimhe. Tá seisear clainne agus ochtar clann clainne acu.

Geraldine Mills

IN A FAR-OFF MAYFLY SEASON

Diggers hulk upon our road on their way
to pile drive another foundation into bog.
Our house shudders and all pictures tilt.

Persimmons fall out of bowls,
wine flows back into jugs, a cat into a gramophone.
Footballs caught in triumph slip out of grasp;
The sleeping maid whose pots and pans slide
into the next room beyond the frame
sink below the rising water table.
.
In a far-off mayfly season a fisherman
will catch his hook in our window frame
and reel in the cleaned bones of it;
he will place it in his boat beside two trout
his box of bait, not knowing

how a man and a woman
their two children, look out at trees
that crouch like a lioness,
a fox blazing against snow
or where they lay their heads at night
she in the curve of his sleep
he closer to the door to protect her.

SETTING: *A middle class suburban kitchen. Chrome, maple cupboards, no expense spared. The sink off-centre back. A window behind it. A door to one side. A table towards the centre front with an aerosol can, silver spoons, a golf trophy, a silver salver, some polish and cloth.*

At RISE: *Rita, a woman in her late thirties/forties, stands at the sink wiping down the draining board, looking out the window. She is wearing leggings and a t-shirt with a sleeveless fleece over it. There is the sound of a cat crying in the background.*

RITA turns to the audience and speaks

Will you listen to the sound of that cat, yowling just because he sees me? You'd think I'd half killed him but he's like that, Herman, such a mean cat. He hates me. He looks at me with a bad eye.

RITA makes a face

Yeah, mean and sly. I bet he's thinking 'I'll make her work for her money today'. And he does you know; he makes life miserable for me.

pointing

There he is now, coming in through the flap in the door, in from the rain that has started to pelt off the new decking they just got. And what will Mrs P do? Oh I know; she'll take down the towel, the one with H monogrammed in blue on it, H for Herman, of course and dry him all over, kissing him and petting him until I want to throw up. 'My ikkle ikkle baby', she'll croon, 'my gorgeous boy'.

RITA moves to the fridge, takes out a carton of milk, pours it into a bowl, places it in the microwave, switches it on

And it's the same order every day 'Warm some milk for my precious, Rita, before you do the bedrooms or the living room or the conservatory'.

Sound of microwave ping, RITA takes out the bowl, exits, returns

You should see him; the way that fat cat waits until I pour the warmed milk into his bowl. Then he'll crouch at its rim, touch it with his paw, put out his tongue to check its temperature, make sure I've got it right, before he'll drink it. While he's drinking, Mrs P gets ready for work. She thinks I'm great, always singing my praises. Says I'm her little treasure. That's me, Rita her woman who does two days a week. I come just ten minutes before she's heading off and she has a list ready for me.

RITA lists them off on her fingers

Scrub the tiles behind the cooker, pull out fridge, dust the videos, look after Herman. 'No bother', I lie, 'of course I'll air his basket'. She makes me polish his scratching post and his mean eye slants at me while I rub the polishing cloth up and down. He walks around as if he owns the blooming place, rubbing his back along the couches of cream leather. Every day it's the same. I finish off washing the white marble floor and he walks across it in his milk-bloated bones leaving a trail of paw prints on it out of pure cat spite. Then he walks back along the corridor to Mrs P's bedroom as she gets ready. He slinks between her legs as she puts on her earrings. She gives a little cry of pleasure like she just had her fanny tickled and I can picture her picking him up and kissing him.

RITA pouts her lips in a kiss, and makes kissing noises

Bet she prefers him to fat-faced Mr P with his ugly hands and his red boozer's nose.

RITA moves to empty the dishwasher, taking out plates and cups putting them on the shelves above her. Sound of a car driving away

There, she's gone now, out the driveway in a Gucci rush. Great. I always have to wait until I can no longer hear the car and then it's my chance.

RITA exits. There is the sound of a door opening. a cat screeching. She returns smiling

Well that's him out of the way.

SHE whispers

I've moved the bin in front of the cat flap so that he can't get back in. Let him yowl and scrape all he likes. He's not getting back in to put his filthy cat hairs all over the place after me cleaning it.

RITA sits down at the table and takes out her cigarettes During the following, she lights up and smokes

Mrs P doesn't allow smoking in her house. But she'll never know. A little spray here, a little spray there and I'll have it smelling country fresh by the time she comes home.

(beat)

You know, all the houses I do for are different. The women have different names for me: Mrs Mop, My Little Treasure, My Cleaning Lady. I am their status symbol, like the golf club, their American Express Gold. Jack, that's my husband, gives out, saying I shouldn't be skivvying for the likes of them because they don't give a shit about me with their fancy high-powered jobs, their I-pods. He doesn't realise that if it wasn't for me they'd be living like sluts. Look at Mrs Higgins. I do for her on Tuesdays and Thursdays. She swans around in her tinted eyebrows, French polished nails, and she leaves her bedroom like a pig sty. Dirty knickers and tights thrown all over the floor. Coffee cups congealed. One time I even found an orange in the bottom of her wardrobe, growing little green tufts of hair, it was there so long. Honest. And the smell, it nearly brought on an attack of my asthma. But you should just see her wash basin in the en-suite. Each time I go there I spend the best part of my time scraping off the slime of mascara and makeup glued to her gold taps. Far from gold taps she was reared. She says she cannot do without me either, but she looks down on me. I know. I can tell these things. I can hear her at her dinner parties, talking about me, as she sips her Chardonnay. How good I am, but common, common as muck. She thinks she's real smart but she's not. I tell her there's a blue-bottle fly after landing on the cooked chicken and she tells me to throw it in the bin. Me and Jack have a great laugh as we pull its wish bone for our supper and we watching 'Fair City'. The only thing in her favour is that she doesn't have a cat. Will you listen to him, still whinging outside the door?

Sound of cat crying

God, you couldn't get any work done with that.

She turns on the radio. The room fills with a chat-show programme.

I love, just love, the Gerry Ryan programme. Isn't he gorgeous with them luscious lips and his sexy voice. And as for the people he interviews, Jeez they're the business; only last week he had a woman on, whose husband fell in love with her gay brother. The poor woman, she was in bits, she was. She didn't know whether she was Arthur or Martha with all the carry on. Haven't some people terrible lives too? But I don't let it get in on me. So I sing along with the songs he plays while I'm cleaning, Robbie Williams, Westlife, Sting, *Roxanne you don't have to put on your red dress ...*

RITA dances around singing into an aerosol can she has taken from the table

It's a lovely song isn't it, and Sting, he's real easy on the eye. But he's a bit too kinky for my liking. You know all that tantric stuff. I prefer my man a bit more, you know missionary. That's what I love about my Jack, he's the real thing, not like Mr P himself. That pervert cornered me once when I was bending over the loo cleaning their filth. 'You could do with a bit of real Mr Muscle', he says to me, his hand coming in between my legs. I just had enough time to swing the Toilet Duck back on him and got the front of his nice new Louis Copeland suit. 'Bitch', he growled after me as I turned and took my cleaning stuff off down the hall, but did I care? Still I don't like being around him, or the cat. They both look at me with the same eye. I don't know which is worse.

RITA stubs out her cigarette, picks up the aerosol and walks around spraying the room.

Now that should do it. It smells like the Botanical Gardens.

RITA puts the cigarette box with the ash in to her pocket

Sometimes I get too tired to do all the work Mrs P leaves for me. So I go through the laundry basket and any thing that looks clean I give a little spray of Febreze, run the iron over it and Bob's your uncle. Or your aunt if you're on Gerry Ryan's show. And the funny thing is, she's never any the wiser.

She leaves down the aerosol and starts polishing some silver she has waiting: spoons, a golf trophy, a silver salver

But I like Mrs Collins, I do for her after Mrs P. Now she's a lady. She cleans before I come, has the ironing sorted. So that it's whites Monday, coloureds Wednesday. We have a cup of tea while she admires her washing flap away in the breeze. She takes out the shortbread. We have two pieces each before she puts the tin away. She asks about Jack and I tell her about the blouse he just bought me. She tells me I'm very lucky with my man and that she looks forward to me coming. You know I think I break up the empty day for her. Someone she can talk to.

But The Perverts I don't like them and I'll tell you why. You see, Mr P bought Mrs P a new ring. She flashed it at me as I was changing her Egyptian cotton sheets. 'It's an emerald', she gloated. 'He brought it back from his foreign travels. He went up to a small mine in one of the mountains and chose it all by himself. It's such a good emerald', she said, brandishing it under my nose. 'look, it's as clear as water'. I looked, she was right. The light went right through the jewel. But I saw a programme on the Discovery channel only last month about precious stones. I remember they said that an emerald has to be a bit cloudy to prove it's the real McCoy. But hers was crystal clear. I laughed inside knowing she's a fool, and as for him, I'm only sorry I didn't do more damage with the Toilet Duck. Jeez, I could murder a cup of coffee,

RITA gets up, fills a cup from the cafétiere, brings over the biscuit tin, rummages through until she gets one she likes, bites into it.

As I was saying, The Perverts. I knew as soon as I came in on Wednesday that there was something wrong. There's no 'How's my little treasure this morning'. Her face was like one of them black clouds you see over the heads of mobile phone users in scary ads. She was, as you might say, giving off dangerous radiation.

'My emerald', she said, 'is missing'.

'Your bit of glass', is what I wanted to say, but instead I cried, 'Oh my God'.

'You haven't seen it'.

'And why would I?' said I.

'Well I showed it to you on Monday and I haven't seen it since'.

'If you didn't make such a mess, Mrs Pervert', I wanted to scream at her, but of course I didn't. Instead, I said 'I'll help you look for it'.

So I pulled out lockers, cleaned behind them, poured out the wastepaper basket, checked even the drum of the washing machine. Nothing. We pulled everything apart. When we had all but given up hope I gave one last shake to Herman's blanket. And yes, you've guessed it, a glittering circle tinkled to the floor. I looked at the cat. He just sat on the table washing his face, as innocent as anything, the underside of his paw showing.

There was an extra tenner in my money envelope that week. I don't look a gift horse in the mouth. But I don't forget either.

You see, Jack said there was a going away do in the job. Mr Matthews retiring you know. There was going to be loads of food, free booze all night. I didn't have anything to wear so I went and had a look see in Mrs P's wardrobe. There was a lovely slinky dress, blue with spaghetti straps like something Liz Hurley would wear to a film premiere. I looked at the label on it. It must have cost hundreds, thousands even. I tried it on in front of her feng shui mirror. Even if I say so myself, I looked gorgeous. She hadn't worn it yet. She got it for one of her school friend's wedding who's marrying some high falutin' company director. There was a lovely Prada handbag and shoes to match. Herman was outside at the time, stuck against the window, glaring. He screeched at me as I carefully packed up the dress and the bits and pieces into my own bag. And do you know what struck me? For all their money they don't have much of a life. For all their fancy couches and leather chairs they haven't a place they can cuddle up to one another and drink cider in front of the fire like me and my Jack. Who'd want that? Anyway the dress. We had a brilliant night. Everyone said I looked gorgeous. Where did I get it, they all wanted to know? I made up a story about my mother getting a bag of clothes from the Oxfam Shop and it was in it. Shoes and all? Yeah, I laughed, isn't it the business. Anyway we are dancing away to Chris de Burgh, Jack singing in my ear, 'Lady in blue is dancing with me, cheek to cheek' when he whispers that he can't wait to get the dress off me.

RITA stands and starts to dance around the kitchen She continues to dance and hum, reliving the night, running her hands up her thighs, her waist, caressing her shoulders, raising her hands as if slipping the dress over her head.

Very carefully, I caution him, my arms tight around him, thinking of our sagging sofa in front of the fire, his breath hot on my neck, his hands ever so slowly moving the soft blue up over my legs, my thighs. Oh, yes, please Jack, yes, yes, please.

Geraldine Mills writes poetry and short stories. She won the Hennessy New Irish Writer Award in 2000, and came second in the Francis MacManus Award in March 2005. She has published two collections of poetry, *Unearthing Your Own* (Bradshaw 2001) and *Toil the Dark Harvest* (Bradshaw 2004). *This is From the Woman who Does* was shortlisted for the Francis Mac Manus Award in 2003, and was selected as the only international entry for the Provincetown Women Playwrights' Festival, Mass. USA in October 2004.

FAUSTUS AR AN DRABHLÁS

tic teaic, tic teaic, tic teaic ...

Mhothaigh sé an tic teaic ag snámh
Ar a chraiceann, á chur faoi luí na bíse -

Cad a chlog é? Cad a chlog é?

Ón uair a d'ardaigh Mephistophiles barr a mhéire
Ina threo agus cromruathar dearg air,
Thosaigh an bás ag támáil a bheola, ag tarraingt
Sceith an mheisce as a bhéal leibideach.

Faustus bocht ag cromadh, raiceáilte,
Ragairne a laethanta ag teacht chun críche.

tic teaic, tic teaic, tic teaic ...

I gcuilithe a fhiabhrais, ceap sé aingeal geal
Ag teacht faoin a dhéin, á scaoileadh
Ó chrúba an diabhail bhuí, á shábháil as íochtar ifrinn -

Faustus bocht ina chrunca gúngach, ag rámhaille
In a lándhúiseacht

(An aingeal dubh thar a ghualainn)

Faustus bocht i meá an bháis, a rith baoise
Beagnach thart,

Fear na gcrúb ag frimhagadh
tic teaic, tic teaic, tic teaic, tic ...

Bhí an ghrian ag brath ar a dhul faoi
Nuair a dhruid ógfhear saolta isteach

Ar thaobh an locha, snámh na lánghealaí
Ar intinn aige - agus briseadh

As a stadsmaoineamh í, síofra locha
Ag rianú uisce na gcloch in íochtar

Na roschoille. Sailm fir ní ba bhreátha
Ní fhaca sí riamh in a chraiceann dearg, ní ba

Ghile agus é ag treabhadh na scairbhe; seoid
Fir a chuir port ina cuid fiacal,

Uisce na locha ag lupadáil, lapadáil.

...

Bhí na réalta ag spréacharnaigh
Nuair a d'imigh sí in éineacht leis -
(Uisce na locha ag lupadáil, lapadáil)
Gan bac ar an scaollscáth a chlúdaigh

An ghealach nó ar uiscefhocla a hathar:
Thar do bhaint, thar do bhaint.

Go dtí gur shroich sí talamh na mbacach,
Go bhfuair sí í féin ar an uaigneas

Ag gliúmáil síos siar san uisce, go dtí
Gur mheall sí é go grinneall locha,

Níor fhill sí ar a cine faoi thoinn.

Ar mhullach a dhá ghlúin a bhí sé
Nuair a bhuail spiach spéire é,

Aibhse na coirbe diaga
Tagtha aniar adhuaidh air,

Gan fiú focal faire, gan fáth.

In ainneoin a raibh caillte aige -
A thalamh, a chuid, a chlann,
An smior as na cnámha, chloígh sé

Leis an Dia nach dtréigeann.

I bpolláin coipithe an dúfhocail
A fheicimse do ghrian is do ghealach,
Réalta urraithe do shúl,

Mar is eol dom go maireann tú.

I gcomhairle na gcarad, níl le fáil
Ann ach mo lochtsa, cúis mo chiaptha
Leagtha i mbéal mo dhorais,

Ach, gabh i leith ...

Tá a fhios go maith agatsa
Go raibh mise riamh agus choíche
Ar thaobh na n-aingeal,
Ar thaobh mhaithe do ríochta.

Anois, agus mé i mbráca, tá
Do dhuibheagán ag dorchú orm, ag
Cur caille ar láchaint na maidine,
As a lonraíonn aghaidh sciamhach Dé.

ETTY HILLESUM - CÍN LAE, 1943

Fiú amháin in Auschwitz, príomhchathair
Na h-aimhleasa, ag deireadh lae,

Anseo láithreach insna críocha déanacha
I gcroílár dhubhfhocail an chéasta,

Bímse ag spágáil amach romham
Faoi chamscáth na sreinge deilgní,

Scéal earraigh i mo chéim is port úrnua
Leathchumtha i ndúrún mo chroí.

Agus cad chuige nach mbéinn?

Nár mhothaíos Cách ag teacht
I dtalamh i m'aigne? Nach bhfacas

Chugam an Slánaitheoir in áilleacht
An lagsholais; nár airíos

A lámh i mo láimhsa; é ar gábhair
Chun cónásc a dhéanamh

Le saor chomh maith le daor, an mámh
A bhaint as an drámh, mé féin

San áireamh? Cén fáth nach mbeadh
Cuma na meidhre orm?

PROMETHEUS SA BHEARNA

An t-aon sáil coise *Achilles* a bhí aige
Ná blas na báíochta don chine daonna,
Dath a bhí in easnamh i measc na ndéithe eile.

Ina aineoinn sin is uile, thairg sé
Do chré an duine, na tíolachtaí is finne -

Aibhleog dhearg ar an teallach,
Léarscáilíocht na réalta,
Éigse den tseandéanamh,
Leigheaslusanna dá rogha.

An tuairisc curtha aige, mhothaigh sé
An t-uaigneas ag teacht anuas air,

An t-uaigneas céanna a thit ar Chríost
Nuair a leag bean lagmhisniúil
Lámh air, biseach á fháil ón tadhall sabhála.

I ngeall ar a pheaca, tharraing sé an drochshúil
Ar a cheann, ordóg an bháis ar a chéird dhiaga.

Iolar do mo phlacadh,
Loscadh gréine do mo sciúirsadh,
Sioc na hoíche do mo chiapadh,
Ifreann síoraí do mo chéasadh.

Gan faoiseamh, gan sólás, gan guidhe an bháis.
Gan spás sa teampall choíche.

Is file dhátheangach í **Dolores Stewart**. Foilsíodh *In out of the Rain* ag Dedalus (1999), *'Sé Sin Le Rá* (2001) agus *An Cosán Dearg* (2003) ag Coiscéim. Tá bailiúchan nua leí *Presence of Mind* ag teacht ó Dedalus. Chomh maith le sin, scríobhann sí gearrscéalta agus ficsean na bpáisti. Bhuaigh sí an chéad duais i mbéarla agus an dara duais i ngaeilge ag Féile Filíochta Dún Laoghaire/Rath Domhnach (2003), an dara duais i nGaeilge ag Comórtas Filíochta Samhain Smurfit 2003 agus i mBéal Átha na mBuillí, 2004.

ALICE

The room was a suntrap. Sprawled across her bed, Alice wallowed in the muggy heat. Too hot, almost. A black speck on the curtains took flight, collided with a pane of glass. Trapped too, unless she opened a window. Buzzzz, buzzzz. Hard to believe something so small could make such a racket. Someone had told her a joke once about people eating flies. If she were locked in the room, without food, would she stalk the insect? Squash it with a finger? Eat it? No, they'd die together, the fly squat on her cheek, her final companion. Sometimes it was nice imagining herself dead. Dying anyway.

'What are you doing, lying there with your uniform on?' her mother materialized in front of her.

'Thinking', Alice answered.

'Well, think outside. All that lovely weather going to waste'.

'But -'

'No buts. And open a window'.

If her mother were dead would she eat her? Unbuttoning her uniform, Alice shuddered away the thought.

Jelly on the plate, jelly on the plate
Wibbly wobbly, wibbly wobbly
Jelly on the plate.

Alice peered. It seemed miles to where Regina and the rest of her gang were skipping. Why couldn't she stay home? There was no law saying you had to go out. And the dress she'd changed into made her feel as if she might blow away. It let the sun and wind at her. The elements, different from what was in a kettle. 'Cover the element', her mother would shout. Otherwise the kettle might burn. Would it explode in a ball of flames? Burn the house down? For a moment the kettle blazed, tendrils of fire sprouting like the trailing roots of her mother's spider plant.

'Alice, Alice!' Regina's voice carried.

Alice wished the ground would open up and swallow her. But she was so big. Bigger than the houses, bigger than the road, her head touched the sky. She felt her face burn. Like the inside of a kettle when there wasn't enough water.

'Alice, c'mere!'

Inching her way along the road she had the strangest sensation of growing smaller and smaller; while the other girls grew bigger and bigger.

'Hold the rope, you can have a turn later'.

Alice pretended not to see the smirk on Yvonne's face that said she wouldn't get a go later, that when it came to her turn, they'd stop, invent another game. The swishing sound, the sing-song chant, the blurred words of the skipping rhymes, lulled her. It was nice playing, even if it was only pretend.

I had a little dolly,
I left it on the shelf,
Would you believe, would you believe,
It walked away itself.

The rope caught Regina's leg.

'You did that!' the girl flamed.

'What?' Alice faltered.

'Held the rope too tight'.

Spiteful smiles cracked her playmates' reddened cheeks, flickered in their puffed-out eyes. 'You - made - me - out -', Regina prodded the younger girl's chest.

Alice bit her lip.

'Cry-baby!' her tormentor exulted, dancing with glee. 'Cry-baby, cry-baby', the others yelled, howling and spitting in delight.

'I am not', Alice hissed, tears wetting her face.

'Who wants to play with you anyway?' Regina's mouth curved. 'C'mon, let's go to my house'.

Nose in the air, she led the way, the others following in mock procession. Alice watched them flounce up the road. Then she blinked and they disappeared.

Alice ventured into the half-finished housing estate, her eyes on sticks for grown-ups. She'd been warned about going there but if she went home early her mother would blame her for not knowing how to play, for being too sensitive. Sensitive. She'd seen the word on a tube of sun-cream. For skin that burned easily. Would she burn easily? Her eyes burnt, smarted with unshed tears. Tip-toeing through a gap in one of the houses, she found herself in a maze of rooms, each the same as the next, floors carpeted with fuzzy-headed dandelions. Clean up that mess, a voice in her head shrilled. Alice scattered the weeds, gazing in awe as seed-heads rose in a cloud, like snow falling upwards.

'One o'clock, two o'clock', she chanted, wind-milling through the fairy clocks. Eerily, they swarmed round her, attaching themselves to her clothes, her hair, drifting into her mouth. Swatting them away, Alice fled from the room, down a long, narrow corridor. Reaching a back door, she skidded to a halt, her feet teetering at the edge of an enormous crater. With a whoop, she plunged into the brown, clammy earth.

The hole had a tunnel at one end. Near the entrance an enormous granite slab stood guard. Marching up, Alice saluted. Hundreds of tiny, glassy eyes glinted back. 'May I?' she joked, ducking past the stone. A clayey smell filled her nostrils as the dark shell closed over her. When she'd ventured as far as she dared, she hunkered down, wrapping her arms around herself for warmth, resting her head on her knees. A tear trickled down her face. Opening her mouth she caught it with her tongue. It tasted salty. From far away, came the sound of voices. Squeals. Regina's mother must have shooed them out. Alice closed her eyes. If they found her here, Regina would claim the tunnel, do 'one potato, two', make sure she won. She always did. Even when they played tag, Regina was never 'it'. And the time they'd cooked potatoes, she'd eaten all the good ones, left the burnt ones for everyone else. Fingers in her ears, Alice rocked. She'd die rather than let them find the tunnel.

Alice fumbled for the bedside lamp, screaming as her fingers touched something slimy, crumbly. Shooting up, her head bumped the ceiling. Where was she! Where? She was still in the tunnel, that's where she was. She must have fallen asleep. Skin crawling, she groped her way along the damp, oozy earth. At last, her hands felt something solid, rough. The stone, she'd reached the stone! In the sky, stars twinkled. Oh no! Her parents would kill her. Where did they think she was? Why weren't they out looking for her? A scurrying noise made her cry out. She clutched a hand to her mouth, afraid of drawing whatever it was towards her. A mouse, she hoped, not a rat. A murderer, a voice in her head taunted. Not a murderer, she was too young. Terrified, Alice curled into a ball, gritting her teeth as pins and needles attacked her legs. A scream cut the night. Alice heard it. She tried to stop the sound but it was too late. Now she'd started she couldn't stop. On and on she shrieked. She didn't care if someone killed her. She wanted someone, anyone, she didn't want to be alone a second longer.

Light.

Light coming in her direction. Voices.

'Aliiice! Aliiice!!! Are you there? Alice? Answer!'

Torches flashed like cats' eyes.

'Mammeee, Daddeee', she cried.

'Oh thank God, thank God!' her mother answered, dazzling her with light.

'It's her, it's her, it's Alice!' people chorused. A cheer went up. Another. She recognised some of the adults: Regina's father, Yvonne's brother, people from next door. Her mother's arms loomed, pressed her close. She could feel tears, hot against her cold cheeks.

'My little girl', her father crooned, hoisting her on his shoulders, his voice so soft Alice thought it might break.

For a few days Alice was a heroine: kids pointed, whispered. But it was wearing off. That lunchtime when Regina had shouted, 'Go back to the dirty hole you crawled out of', everyone in the playground had laughed. They hadn't laughed the other night, Alice thought, slipping through the makeshift gates into the housing estate. They'd cheered. Reliving the memory, her body glowed as if she was sitting in front of a warm fire, could feel its breath on her skin.

'Look what the cat dragged in'.

Seeing Regina, Alice's mind somersaulted.

'You're not allowed here, your mammy said, so go home', Regina gloated, her face red from dragging a sheet of corrugated iron.

'What are you doing with that corry?' Alice demanded.

Yvonne's head popped out of the tunnel. 'We're making a den. We've got cushions and a carpet'.

'The tunnel's mine, I found it'.

'Excuse me! Did anyone see Alice's name on the door?' Regina scoffed. 'Better go and see your solicitor'.

Alice went hot, cold, stared at the ground. When she glanced up, the other girl had a fishy grin on her face. 'You can come in if you bring something'.

'What?' Alice asked, smelling a rat.

'We're making food but we haven't any matches. You can go to your house and get some'.

Alice nodded. She'd have to be careful, if her mammy found out there'd be murder.

Regina struck a match. The wick in the primus flared, went out. She struck another. This time it held a few moments.

'It's probably wet', Trish sighed.

'Too windy, there's a draught coming in'.

'We could use the corry for a door', Yvonne suggested.

'We won't be able to see'.

'Course we will, with the stove'.

'Alice, put the corry against the door'.

'Why me?'

'Last in, that's why. You know the rules'.

'Smell's gone', Yvonne shouted.

Alice heaved the corrugated iron across the entrance.

'I can't get in', she called.

'Penny's dropped', Regina jeered. 'Who wants you anyway?'

Something hard planted itself in Alice's chest. Everyone wanted her the other night. Everyone. She could hear the girls squabbling, laughing. They'd forgotten her already. 'It's not fair!' she whispered to the stone standing near the mouth of the tunnel. Leaning against it she felt the hardness inside grow and wondered if people could turn into stone. As her fingers traced the glittering sequins on the granite surface, small glassy eyes winked back. We're your friends, they seemed to say, we can help.

Alice pushed and pushed. The ground near the entrance to the tunnel sloped. If she could just dislodge the stone it might topple. Pressing her back against a wall of earth, she used her feet. The stone swayed, rocked, finally tipped over. Now she'd make them suffer. Now they'd have to beg her. Serve them right! Impatiently, she waited for the high-pitched voices to stop, for one of them to notice. As time passed she began to feel uneasy. What possessed her do such a thing? She'd never be able to remove the stone on her own. And if Regina told, there'd be real trouble. From inside the tunnel came a whiff of burning. Alice's throat dried. Better scram; say she went home straightaway. Voices were calling now, yelling. Sweat broke out on her forehead as she raced through the empty house. There was nothing to worry about: they'd probably burned potatoes like last time.

She could still hear them at the gates. The screams reminded her of cheers. The cheers for her. The further away she got, the louder they seemed; screams and cheers fused until she couldn't tell which was which. Through misted eyes, she saw the bright faces of her mother and father, her neighbours. Cheering her. They loved her, really. Loved her. She wouldn't go back. Wouldn't even look back. Let them scream all they wanted.

'Aliiiiiccce, Aliiiiicce, Alliiiiicce!'

Let them scream.

Let them.

Moya Roddy's novel *The Long Way Home* (Attic) was described as 'simply brilliant' in *The Irish Times*. Her work has been anthologized by Penguin, Michael Joseph and Serpent's Tail and broadcast on RTÉ and CBC (Canada). *Dance, Ballerina, Dance*, a radio play, was shortlisted for the P.J. O'Connor Award and broadcast on RTÉ. Moya has written a four-part series for Channel Four, adapted two novels for the screen, and been commissioned to write several screenplays. She is currently finishing a collection of short stories.

Mary O'Rourke

SURVIVAL

Violent sky.
We had longed
for the clouds to burst,
drench our starved earth.
The deluge came
cracking the scorched ground,
slowly seeping through.
We welcomed the stranger
children clasped mothers,
they had never seen rain
they rolled in the mud
sensuous pleasure.

The older ones gazed from their huts
hands held out in reverence
at this gift from Heaven.
They had half-despaired, half-hoped
for a harvest in their lifetime.
Earth steaming before them
smelled of former times
when abundant rains
nourished the earth.

Long into the night
we danced, beat drums, chanted,
then slumbered in deep bliss
'til we awoke
to merciless floods
rising above the village.
Some had perished in the night.
Struggling up the hill,
daring to hope for survival,
we abandoned our homes.

Deceived, dejected
we sought help in nearby towns.

Returned when the rains ceased,
rebuilt our lives
struggled, toiled
sowed crops with aching limbs
watched the green shoots sprouting
daily we measured the growth
slow, steady.
From spring till autumn we dreamed of the harvest,
till the golden ears dazzled our eyes.

ENTRANCE, REGIONAL HOSPITAL

A father counts the hours
His son will spend in theatre
Stabbed in a drugs feud

A spotty teenager checks his watch
As he prepares for three hours on dialysis
Hopes his third kidney transplant
Will soon become a reality

The man with the haemorrhage behind his eye
Hides his cigarettes in a coloured handkerchief
As he escapes the hospital's no smoking zone

Inside, patients' slippered feet
Shuffle along corridors
Nurses move hurriedly from bed to bed
Surgeons call for scalpels
Babies are born, old men die

Here and there someone stops to
Admire the permanent art exhibition.

The whole breath, abdominal, thoracic, clavicular,
Outside the strains of a Bob Dylan busker,
For the times they are a-changing.
Up on all fours, do the cat posture, inhale, stretch,
Exhale, and it's a hard, it's a hard, it's a hard rain's
gonna fall.
Stretch out on bright orange mats,
Focus on the voice, listen, learn.
The songs outside call
Free the mind more than postures or breath.
It's all in the breath, and he knows it.
The breath, the essence,
The air in the song,
The air in the lung.
Breath, air.
He sings easily,
Balancing tone and tune.
Inside I try to balance on one leg,
Failing each time.
Body rhythm, Dylan rhythm,
The answers, my friend, are blowin' in the wind.
Breath, air, wind, balance, rhythm,
Essentials.
Now we'll do the rock 'n' roll position.
It's all in the rock 'n' roll.

Mary O'Rourke was born in Co. Laois, but has lived mainly in Galway, apart from time spent in Mayo, Spain and Germany. She studied languages at UCG. For several years she was involved with An Taibhdhearc and the Patrician Musical Society. Her work is widely published. Her poetry collections, *My Mirror was Cracked* (1999) and *It's all happening* (2004) were published by GMIT, where she works. She is a member of the Galway Writers' Workshop.

Nuala Ní Chonchúir

CLEAMHNAS, 1933

Thug sé dom prátaí:
cnapáin agus póiríní,
iad mór agus beag,
iad crua agus bog.

Thug sé dom poitín
a las tine i mo ghoile,
ach a rinne an luí leis
abhairín níos eascaí.

Thug sé leis clann:
péire leath-fhásta,
iad cúthalach, béasach,
páistí a chéad ghrá.

Thug sé dom báibín,
a d'fhás faoi m'aprún,
sular fhág mé m'athair,
mé soineanta, solúbtha.

Thug sé dom prátaí,
chomh bán leis an ngealach,
chomh buí le turnapa,
iad searbh agus nimhneach.

Níor thug sé dom
ach meas madra.

My name is Caroline Crachami. That is a lie. My name is really Caroline Fogle. I measure one foot ten and a half inches from the top of my skull to the tips of my tippy-toes. One foot. Ten and a half inches. Some people call me The Sicilian Fairy, but I'm not from Italy; I'm from Mallow, which is in County Cork, which is right down the bottom of Ireland. And I'm not a fairy either.

My skeleton stands in a glass box in a museum in London; just the frame of pale bones that used to hold up my skin - that's all that's left of me now. On the floor below my skeleton is another box with a glass lid. This box holds my ruby ring, the grey shoes with black bows, my death-mask, a pair of socks and wax casts of my foot and arm. They are there to prove I was alive once.

The Giant Byrne lives in the glass cabinet beside mine; I don't know what size he is but he is very, very tall. We're a right pair - Ireland's biggest and smallest - one huge brown skeleton beside a tiny white one; two natural freaks. Some people say I'm the teeniest person that ever was; a lot of them used to like to pay two and six to come and look at me at twenty-two New Bond Street. It cost an extra shilling to pick me up and handle me.

My Mama and Dada sold me to Dr. Gilligan; I cost twenty pounds. Dada handed me to Dr. Gilligan on Patrick Street, outside a baker's shop that smelt lovely. We were on a day out in Cork city; that's what Dada said, we were having a day out. Dr. Gilligan met us in the street; he had been to our house to see me but I was asleep that day, tired out from coughing again. Outside the bakery, with cake smells clouding over us, Mama stared at Dr. Gilligan and she wiped away snot and tears from her face with her sleeve, but she never looked at me. I looked at her.

'Mama', I said. My voice is thin and squeaky and sometimes people can't hear me, so I called her again, louder this time: 'Mama'.

She walked away. Dr. Gilligan held me too tight - squeezing me through my clothes - and he made a gurgly laugh. His breath smelt like meat.

'Come now, Caroline my dear', he said and kissed me with his flabby lips, half on my mouth. That left a wet patch on me and I rubbed it away with my fingers.

He brought me on the big boat to England; the boat dropped and lifted in the sea and I felt sick and called for Mama. Dr. Gilligan locked the cabin door and lifted me up onto the high bed; I sat there. He licked his lips and said, 'Well, well'. He picked at my clothes with his hands until they were all off me. Then he tipped me with his cold fingers and laughed; his face got red and he coodled like a pigeon and shook himself. I felt cold.

In London I got new clothes and an old man made them for me and they were lady's clothes. The man stood me on a big wooden table and measured me with a tape and he said, 'How lovely you are' and he was a nice old man. And the clothes he gave me were beautiful: a shiny black dress with a ruffly-puffly white collar and a blue velvet dress with slim sleeves. In another shop I got a hat with a feather and golden earrings and I felt happy, but very tired.

Dr. Gilligan brought me around to see all the people in Liverpool and Oxford and Birmingham. I had my own wooden caravan - painted in gay greens and reds - and the people paid in to meet me. The ladies didn't like me much, they turned their noses away from me, but the men liked me. So I would laugh for them and smile; then they laughed too and felt nice. They liked the way I walked, a bit wobbly and slow, and sometimes they would bend down and take my hand and kiss it. Then they would give me biscuits and - because I was called The Sicilian Fairy - Dr. Gilligan taught me to say thank you in Italian, which was 'Grázie'. I would eat the biscuits and say 'Yum-yum'. Everyone would laugh again and clap their hands for me; all for me. Sometimes my neck felt tight and I would cough and have to have a little rest against the pillows on the caravan's bed, before meeting more people.

Dr. Gilligan brought me to see The King - King George the Fourth - in his home, which was called Carlton House, and I got a new red dress and the ruby ring that's in the glass case on the floor now. It was a special occasion. When we were brought in, I curtsied to The King; his mouth made an 'o' shape and he pulled his breath in through his teeth like a cold wind.

'Good Day, King Number Four', I said, in a posh voice. All the people stared at me, the ladies waggled their heads at each other and some of them looked away.

'King Number Four', The King hootled and he let out a big roaring laugh and then everyone else did the same. I curtsied again and Dr. Gilligan lifted me up and said, 'Well done, my girl', close into my ear. He sat me up on The King's lap and it was funny, because King George was fat and he had lovely soft curly hair, but no crown.

'Caroline was the name of my second wife', The King said, 'but, Miss Crachami, you are more queenly than she could ever have hoped to be'.

Everyone laughed again and nodded to each other and he tickled my chin. Then I started to cough and cough and my eyes felt hot and choky; they got full of tears and I swiped them away with my handkerchief. The King handed me back to Dr. Gilligan who said, 'There, there, Caroline, breathe deeply, my dear', and I tried to get breaths, but I only coughed more.

Little people are better than big people; they take up less room. Small hands and feet are nicer than big ones; they are dainty, Dr. Gilligan said. Men like small ladies better than big ones, even when they only have a tiny bosom. Small ladies like big men, except when they hurt them with their fingers and hands. Big ladies don't like little ladies, they don't think men should like them so much and they are jealous of their daintiness and their tinkly laughs and how they fit in small spaces. Big ladies have loud laughs - they go ha-ha-ha - that shake all their bodies and make their faces red like turkeys.

The day after visiting The King I felt tired and every day after that again I felt more and more sleepy. I cried for my Mama and Dada in the night time and in the day time. Dr. Gilligan told me to stop all my nonsense because I was giving myself puffy eyes and a bedraggled air. My throat felt raggy and blood came onto my hanky every time I coughed. I just wanted to lie down, but Dr. Gilligan said, 'No, no, you have important business to attend to, young lady'. He helped me to get dressed.

I wanted to go home to Mallow; I wanted to take the big boat back across the sea to my own place. Even though I was sick, Dr. Gilligan didn't give me any medicines; he didn't even have a black bag. When my coughing got too bad, my Mama used to hold my head over a bowl of boiled-up water that had a minty smell. She would cover my head with a cloth and put the bowl under my face and tell me to breathe from the bottom of my belly. She rubbed my back. Dr. Gilligan didn't do that. He got angry with me and told me to buck up; he rouged my cheeks and said I was to smile.

On my last day I sat on the bed in the caravan, waiting to talk to the people who wanted to see me. My breath rootled and rattled in my throat like a clatter of old spoons; I felt hot and weak. I cried a lot.

'Please let me go home', I said, 'please, Doctor, please let me'.

'Oh, not this bloody nonsense again'. He stared down at me and poked at his teeth with one nail. He found something stuck there and lifted it close to his eyes to look at it. Then he popped it back in his mouth. I coughed and coughed; it was hacky and sore and blood spluttered onto my dress. 'For goodness sake, Caroline!'

Dr. Gilligan rushed around trying to find something clean for me to wear. He pulled things out of the wardrobe and my trunk, then stuffed them back in. I watched him get angry and throw all my clothes about; I laid my head on the pillows, put my hand to my mouth and died. That made him really annoyed; when he noticed. He shook me a few times and called my name but I was already gone. He put me into his carpet bag and brought me straight to the College of Surgeons and that's where he sold me for a lot more money than he paid to my Dada and Mama.

The surgeons placed me on a marble table and sliced through my skin with a small knife; I was like an apple being cut up for tarts. They looked at all my bits and pieces, lifting them out and writing things about them in a book. Afterwards they put me in a pot and boiled the flesh off my bones until I was the clean skeleton that I am now. They gave me to the museum when I was finished.

Dada came to look for me but he was too late.

Nuala Ní Chonchúir lives in Loughrea. She has won the inaugural Cúirt New Writing Prize (2004), the Francis Mac Manus Award (2002), the Cecil Day Lewis Award (2003), and has twice been nominated for the Hennessy Award (2001 and 2005), all for fiction. Her first collection of short stories *The Wind Across the Grass* was published by Arlen House and her first collection of poetry *Molly's Daughter* appeared in the original ¡DIVAS! anthology. Last year she was awarded an Arts Council Bursary in Literature.

Marion Moynihan

The Moon's Daughter

I am the moon's daughter
I ebb and flow and drown in cycles.

Last night
I talked to my moonsister
told her I hated her
her bitchiness
how nothing is ever right
how she evens scores
takes revenge.
She bears no resemblance to me
though we have the same father
and the same mother.
My mother noticed when I was thirteen
said I was a lovely child ...
until then.

Oh! Goddess of the moon
tonight take a piece of paper
in my planetary colour
light it with a candle
and wait till it burns down.
Persephone, Levanah, Aphrodite,
guide me towards the phase
of sagging breasts and dry vaginas.

I never asked to be young.

FOR MY FIFTY-FIFTH BIRTHDAY

For my fifty-fifth birthday
I *don't* want another leather bag
or a comfortable pair of Ecco shoes
or a hand painted headscarf
or a voucher for a Golden Years' weekend
or even an hour's facial in the Radisson
or a year's subscription to Oprah.

What I *do* want for my fifty-fifth birthday
is a purple butterfly tattooed
between my navel and vagina
so that when the doctor visits
the nursing home in my ninety-fifth year
and everything else is shrivelled
and every faculty faulty or missing
he will know that once there was this woman
with a skittish sense of fun who found love
at fifty-five and marked it with a purple butterfly.

TONGUE TIED

If you ask me once more
if I'd like a cup of tea
I'll scream.

I'll scream so loud
that my tonsils
or what remains of them

will stick to a tree
at the other side of the road
and my tongue

will sit nicely
at the edge of Fenit pier
floodlit by night

and the sound of my scream
will hollow a hole
in the ocean bed

big enough for the two of us
and maybe then you'll know
it's not tea I'm after.

ISSUES

We chatted for hours over tea in Jury's
where he explained the ISEQ, FTSE, NASDAQ
and DOW, for this I will be eternally grateful.
He even held my hand, brushed my cheek leaving.

Last week I asked him to be honest
to let me know if this was going anywhere.
He said he had some issues.
First, there was the question of height
he was six foot one, I was four foot eleven in my socks.
Then there was the question of weight
but we won't go into that.
Then comes the real problem,
the fact that I didn't have
a sustainable income.

Everything in his life fitted into a little box - except me.
Another one not only bites the dust but hopefully
chokes on it.

PAUL DURCAN'S IDEA OF HEAVEN

He's got a headache
he's got it all day.
He watches football on television
I read the Sunday newspapers.
An interview with Paul Durcan
says that Paul's idea of heaven
is finding a compatible woman to live with.
Back to him again
Birmingham didn't win, they drew.
He consults a cookery book
bakes a batch of teacakes
makes me tea
takes a nap
he's still got the headache.
I prepare a pot of Irish stew
we both watch Coronation Street.
After dinner the phone rings
it's one of his women friends
he says, *yes, yes it's fine,*
everything is great.
He becomes animated.
He discusses our trip to Amsterdam,
two for the price of one
with the Quinnsworth tokens.
He told her I was back in Limerick
how we slept in my room
on Friday night in a single bed.
There was a pause at that -
then a laugh.
He told her about his job,
how he loved the kids
and all that technology.
He talked about our new home
and how it was coming along.
Then he tells her he's got to finish the ironing.

He neglected to tell her about the teacakes.
Needless to say, he slept on the couch last night.

THE SIXTIES

I missed the revolution
for me the sex wasn't free,
every month I paid in confession,
every month I got ten Hail Marys
until some guy got wise
and gave me the Stations of the Cross.

Then I started my own revolution,
I stopped going to mass,
I discovered orgasms,
I left my husband,
the one I dressed in white for;
the one I missed the revolution for.

Marion Moynihan is originally from Kanturk, Cork; she completed an MA in Writing at NUIG, and renovated a cottage in Connemara where she now resides with her cat and her computer. Marion studied Creative Writing in Thomas Moore College in Kentucky, where she received an award for editing the college literary magazine *Words*. She has been published in *The Sunday Tribune, Ropes* and the anthologies *Cum, Turbulence* and *The Heart of Kerry*. Her poem, *Paul Durcan's Idea of Heaven,* was featured on RTÉ radio's *The Enchanted Way*. She was short-listed for the Strokestown Prize in 2000, and was the Galway county winner of the Firewords Poetry Award for 2005.

In Ainm an Athar

Dúirt duine críonna liom tráth go bhfuil gach duine mar an gcéanna. Beag, mór, dathúil, gránna, níl ionainn ar fad ach cré. Dúirt sé go bhfuil na tréithe pearsanta céanna ionainn ar fad cé go mbíonn tréith faoi leith chun tosaigh ar thréithe eile ó dhuine go duine. Dúirt sé liom go gcaithfinn mo shaol mar a chaith daoine romham é agus mar a chaithfeadh daoine i mo dhiaidh é. Dúirt sé liom nach mbuailfinn ach le duine amháin i rith mo shaoil a sheasfadh amach ó chuile dhuine eile, duine a d'iompódh mo shaol ar a thóin agus a chuirfeadh ar an treo ceart mé. Ba thráthúil an tairngreacht í.

D'oscail mé doras árasáin J.P. agus chuaigh mé isteach ann. Bhí an áit bánaithe anois. Bhí gach rud glan, néata, in ord is in eagar, agus chuir fuacht na háite uaigní mífháilte romham. Thosaigh mé ag crith agus shamhlaigh mé duine ag damhsa ar m'uaigh. Chuardaigh mé ar an tseilf leabhar sa seomra suite agus fuair mé an rud a bhí uaim. Ar mo bhealach amach dom, thug mé sracfhéachaint ar chlár ama an lae a bhí greamaithe ar chúl an dorais. Clár ama deifnídeach nár athraigh sé riamh, clár ama a thug cur síos ar a shaol aisteach go dtí go ndeachaigh sé thar fóir leis.

5:00 r.n. Paidreacha

7:00 r.n. Leithreas agus Gléasadh

7:10 r.n. Bus

8:00 r.n. Ollscoil

6:00 i.n. Bus

6:50 i.n. Leithreas

6:51 i.n. Duine fiúntach a shábháil

Níor lean mé orm ag léamh. Chroith mé mo cheann le heaspa tuisceana. Chuir mé an glas ar an doras agus shiúil trasna an halla go dtí m'árasán féin, ag cuimhneamh ar an gcéad uair a leag mé súil air, an chéad uair a d'oscail mé doras m'árasáin féin dó, a lig mé isteach i mo shaol é.

Bhí mé díreach tar éis bogadh isteach san áit, agus bhí Cáit is Peadar in éineacht liom, ag crochadh pictiúirí ar na ballaí is ag folmhú na mboscaí móra a tháinig ó Éirinn an lá roimhe. Bhí dorchadas na hoíche ag titim agus ní raibh le cloisteáil ach 'Bang Bang Bang Bang' práinneach an chasúir, sula mbeadh sé ródhorcha leanúint ar aghaidh leis an obair. D'osclaíomar buidéal fíona chun an t-árasán nua a bhaisteadh agus shlogamar siar go gasta é. Leis an mbraon istigh bhí an chiall amuigh, agus thosaigh an chraic is an ceol caochta. Shíl mé gur chuala mé cnag ar an doras agus léim mé i mo sheasamh go fuinniúil, réidh agus lántoilteanach dul i mbun cainte le pé duine nó taibhse a bhí ann.

Francach beag bídeach a bhí ina sheasamh os mo chomhair faoi sholas an halla, agus cé nach ionann Francaigh agus francaigh go hiondúil, bhí an-chosúlacht eatarthu sa chás seo. Nó b'fhéidir go raibh an fíon ag cur dallamullóg orm. Bhí clúmh tiubh fada ar an bhFrancach seo, ag seasamh ar bharr a chinn, spíce i ndiaidh spíce, a chuir túr solais Shráid Uí Chonaill i gcuimhne dom láithreach. Bhí dath an bháis ar a éadan, dath *sel et poivre* ar a chlúmh áiféiseach agus starrfhiacla géara ag lonrú trína mheangadh gáire, mar a bheadh rian na fola fós orthu.

Stán mé air go hamhrasach anois, ag breathnú ar a t-léine dhubh le '√ *Just do it (for Jesus)*' scríofa i litreacha móra bána trasna uirthi. Caithfidh gur cheap sé go raibh sé iontach greannmhar - é sin nó bhí sé corr. Sheas mise an fód tamall, á scrúdú go grinn trí mo shúile caochta.

'Má tá tú i mbun earcaíochta do chreideamh éigin, níl suim agam ann', arsa mise go hairdeallach.

Ach tharraing Peadar isteach san árasán é in éadan mo thola, toisc go bhfaca sé rud nach bhfaca mise in aon chor. Bhí cáca milis i lámh amháin an Fhrancaigh agus an leabhar naofa sa lámh eile, agus ní raibh bealach ní b'fhearr ann le Peadar a mhealladh óir ní raibh greim ite aige ó mhaidin.

Shuíomar ar bhoscaí míchompordacha an oíche sin agus chuireamar aithne ar a chéile. Fuair J.P. coinnle dúinn. Lasamar iad mar ní raibh aon leictreachas ann agus bhreathnaíomar ar an ngileacht ag leathnú ar fud an tseomra. Dúirt J.P. liom gur gearradh an leictreachas toisc gur fhág an mac léinn deireanach a bhí ann an tír gan íoc as a bhille. Níor chuir sin iontas ar bith orm. D'alpamar an cáca milis go craosach, á mholadh go hard as deireadh a chur lenár ngorta mór óir ba throm an t-ualach é an bolg folamh. Labhraíomar faoin leabhar naofa a bhí á chuimilt aige go cúramach ceanúil idir a dhá bhos. Fuair an solas an ceann ab fhearr ar an dorchadas sa leabhar, díreach mar a fuair sé i m'árasán nua agus i saol is in anam J.P.

Bhí Cáit ciúin tamall, ag cur na súl tríd ó bhaithis go bonn. Ansin thosaigh sí á cheistiú, ceist i ndiaidh ceiste, mar a bheadh cluiche fiche ceist ann, chun scrúdú coinsiasa a dhéanamh ar an bhfear beag aisteach a bhí ar a haghaidh amach is é ag brú a bhealaigh isteach inár saol. D'fhreagair sé í mar a bheadh sé ina shuí i gclár na mionn i bpríomhchúirt na Fraince.

D'inis sé scéal a shinsear, scéal a athar *biologique* dúinn an oíche sin i bhFraincis bhreá líofa agus d'éisteamar go géar leis. Níor thuigeamar chuile fhocal dar ndóigh, ach idir an triúr againn, d'éirigh linn an scéal a athchumadh muid féin mar a bheadh preabshábh á chur le chéile againn, píosa i ndiaidh píosa, gach aon phíosa san áit cheart. Thosaíomar á cheistiú.

"Bhfuil tú á rá linn', arsa Peadar i bhFraincis bhriste ólta, 'gur labhair Dia le do dhaidí agus gur éirigh sé as an ngadaíocht is as an troid láithreach?' Lig sé scairt gháire as.

'Tá', arsa J.P., lándáiríre. 'Chonaic sé solas neimhe. Bhí sé ar a aimhleas agus tugtha do hearóin ach, ag an nóiméad sin, stop sé go deo na ndeor'.

'Seans go raibh mearadh air!' arsa Cáit go ciúin ionas nach gcloisfeadh J.P. í.

'Ní raibh', a d'fhreagair J.P., go críonna. 'Míorúilt a bhí ann. D'fhill mo dhaidí ar na siopaí as ar ghoid sé na hearraí éagsúla, agus thug sé ar ais iad. Ghabh sé a leithscéal agus chuaigh sé le sagartóireacht'.

'Ach níl cead ag sagairt pósadh!'

'Sagairt Chaitliceacha, a Cháit', arsa Peadar, agus a cheann á chroitheadh aige. 'A leithéid d'aineolas!'

'Ach más andúileach thú, ní féidir leat éirí as chomh tapaidh sin', a dúirt mé go smaointeach.

Ach níor éist J.P. liom.

'Breathnaíonn sibh ach ní fheiceann sibh. Éisteann sibh ach ní thuigeann sibh', ar sé. Bhí díomá le brath ina chuid cainte. Chreid seisean scéal míorúilte a athar. Chreid sé go raibh sé féin ar an domhan daonna mar thoradh ar an míorúilt úd, agus go raibh sé de dhualgas air na daoine óga Éireannacha seo a tharraingt ar ais ó bhruach ifrinn, lena bpeacaí marfacha a bhain lena ndúil nimhe sa chraic, sa cheol is san ól, a bhí ag creimeadh a n-anama.

Ag 6:51 i.n. lá i ndiaidh lae as sin amach, bhuaileadh J.P. an cnag ceannann céanna ar dhoras m'árasáin. Uaireanta bhínn liom féin, uaireanta eile ní bhínn, ach níor chuir sé sin stop leis. Ba é mo shlánaitheoir é, m'fhuascailteoir pearsanta, a chuirfeadh ar bhealach na fírinne mé - dar leis, ina intinn féin. Ach bhí spraoi agam leis, lena thuairimí aisteacha is scéalta iontacha. Thosaigh sé ar bhealach neamhurchóideach go leor, leis na rudaí beaga dar ndóigh. Chuir sé comórtas ar bun idir mé féin, Peadar is Cáit chun deireadh a chur lenár ndiamhaslú is eascainí. Chuile uair a mhaslaíomar é, chuireamar 10 cent i 'mbosca na bpeacaí', ach chomh luath is a thug J.P. a dhroim linn, bhaineamar amach arís é, chun buidéal fíona eile a cheannach.

Lig Peadar air gur homaighnéasach a bhí ann i gcomhair spraoi, agus ghuigh J.P. ar son míorúilte. B'fhacthas dó go raibh an diabhal ní ba ghaire dúinn ná mar a cheap sé ar an gcéad dul síos, agus leag sé lámh ar chros bheannaithe chun fear na gcrúb a dhíbirt ó chorp Pheadair, ach rith Peadar amach as an bhfoirgneamh sna trithí gáire, mar a bheadh fear na gcrúb féin sa tóir air.

Cé go raibh J.P. mar ionadaí Dé, bhí mothúcháin dhaonna fós aige. Ba léir go raibh uaigneas air. Bhí a athair i bhfad uaidh agus níor chaith na Francaigh eile go maith leis. Ní raibh muinín acu as; bhí sé ródhifriúil, róchráifeach don tír thuata inar chuir sé faoi. Bhí uaigneas air agus bhí cailín uaidh - mar chompánach, mar bhean, mar mháthair dá chlann, óir bhí sé ag teannadh amach sna blianta - bheadh sé fiche bliain d'aois i gceann míosa. Chuala sé faoi mhíorúilt na míorúilte. D'inis sé a phlean dúinn.

'Tá cara agam', a dúirt sé.

Bhí iontas orainn cheana féin.

'Tá cara agam agus phós sé cailín álainn. Bhí sé i ngrá léi le fada ach grá leatromach a bhí ann'.

'Agus?' arsa Peadar go borb.

'Agus ghuigh sé chun Dé. D'inis sé a fhadhb Dó. Labhair Dia leis agus mhol Sé dó troscadh agus guí a dhéanamh ar feadh daichead lá, mar a rinne A mhac féin san fhásach fadó, agus gheobhadh sé a achainí. B'shin a rinne sé agus b'shin a fuair sé, óir d'éist an cailín lena ghuí trí ghuth Dé'.

'Raiméis!' arsa Peadar. 'Má chreideann tú é sin, tá tú as do mheabhair - ach tá tú as do mheabhair ar aon nós'.

'Ní hamháin go gcreidim é', arsa J.P., 'ach tá mé chun an rud céanna a dhéanamh'.

'Ní fhéadfá!' arsa mise, ag briseadh isteach air. Níor éirigh liom fanacht i mo thost. 'Daichead lá - ar son mná! Níl ann ach díth céille! Ní fiú é! Táim cinnte go bhfuil bealach níos fusa, níos réadúla ann chun bean a fháil!'

Ach arís, níor éist J.P.

'B'shin tríocha cúig lá ó shin go baileach', a dúirt mé liom féin go brónach. Cé nach raibh neart agam air, mhothaigh mé ciontach nár éirigh liom stop a chur leis. Chuaigh sé thar fóir an uair seo. Bhí sé de nós aige troscadh chuile dheireadh seachtaine - in ómós do Dhia a dúirt sé, ach níor cheap mé riamh go n-éireodh leis troscadh a dhéanamh ar feadh míosa, gan ach braoinín uisce á ól aige. Níor chnag sé ar dhoras m'árasáin ar feadh an ama sin, d'fhan sé leis féin, ag machnamh, ag guí, ag íobairt a chroí.

Bhí íomhá eile os mo chomhair san ospidéal, íomhá thruamhéalach den phíopa sáite isteach ina bhéal agus bioráin mhóra ag tochailt faoina chraiceann nocht, gan ach seascacht fhuar ina thimpeall. Bhí sé imithe i dtanaíocht, le scíon an bháis ina shúile is dreach an bháis ina ghné Fhrancach. Ba léir go raibh a chinniúint i lámha Dé anois, má bhí nó mura raibh sí riamh roimhe. Bhí a Bhíobla oscailte ar an mbord taobh leis ach bheartaigh mé an leabhar naofa a thóg mé óna árasán a léamh ina áit, an leabhar ina bhfuair an solas an lámh in uachtar ar an dorchadas, an leabhar a thabharfadh sólás neamhdhomhanda dó in am mar seo.

'The Lord of the Rings', a dúirt mé, 'caibidil a haon ...'

Ríona Nic Congáil is from Moycullen, Co. Galway. She is the author of Oireachtas award-winning *An Túr Solais* (Coiscéim 2004) and *The Crystal Tower of Light* (Arlen House 2005).

Una O'Higgins O'Malley

CONNEMARA

It seems that everything that happens here is magnified
Each leaf is twice as green, each spider matters more
Than in the city. There is a sense of taking part in
Ongoing drama or like voyaging
Into unexplored territory.
You feel connected with your being in a deeper, closer,
way
And yet you know there are agendas
Way beyond your own experience
Happening all around you.
I understand now the old belief in fairies;
In this countryside you must make room
For questions greater than yourself.
In the city it is a matter of getting to
The supermarket or the dry-cleaners;
Here those things happen too but they are
Separate.
Always there is a
Sense of otherness, of stronger influence,
Of mystery.

They were taking him to his grave and, quite simply, she did not see how she could live without him. He was her only child, her one support; without him she had nothing and there was no further point in carrying on, in trying to live.

For many grey years she had dreaded this day - ever since she had first wondered if he was involved with the freedom fighters, the resistance movement. Not that she had ever asked him about that. It seemed wiser not to mention her suspicions, because that way they could remain only worries and not facts. He had come and gone from their home in his own time, in his own way. She didn't enquire how he earned the money he gave her weekly; she never commented when unusual things happened, unusual people called. Her own friends, few enough in number, became even fewer; she did not like to invite them often to her home in case, somehow, his secret might be discovered and she didn't delay much talking to them at the market either, because always she felt the need to protect him from the curiosity of others.

Now he was dead, dead from a so-called 'punishment beating' in a laneway not far from where he had lived. The leaden sorrow of his passing was doubled for her by its violence, its stealth.

A crowd of curious onlookers gathered behind her as she walked with his battered remains to the cemetery, but she didn't look round at them. Nor did she look up from behind her draped headscarf when the procession was stopped and a stranger spoke to her - but she *did* see his hand place the hand of her living son in hers. She looked up then into the most loving face she had ever seen and she poured blessings on him again and again for the rest of her lifetime.

FROM PARDON AND FROM PROTEST

I am from heads held high, stiff upper lips
and 'the Clan's' affectionate laughter
where the pain was seldom spoken to the children
- and never among the teacups.

I am from Celtic spirals and the unresolved riddles
of twisted serpents scrolled on holy pages;
I am from dancing-class and make-believe
and graven plaque on cenotaph unheeded.

I am from motherhood and meetings
and an unrelenting trail of grocery trolleys;
I am from history and politics
and letters to the press and pictures of my father.

I am from lines of pilgrims thumbing beads upon their
        journeys,
from surgeon's spattered vests and the near-certainty of
an all-loving Godhead
I am from pardon and from protest - and like the spirals
I return to where I came from.

It isn't comfortable to be revisionist
stare into the eyes of a lost leader
while questioning his values,
take down the busts of heroes from their columns
and lose them in the attics of the memory,
remove their pictures from the walkways of the mind,
pass by their monuments. But it may be
that they were premature in their ambitions;
and when the blood was young and hot, with pulses racing,
they undertook a war of separation
which might have been avoided.

Maybe this blood-stained century
now should be granted leave of absence
or amnestied in mothballs,
and the indomitable Irishry of North and South
should gaze into the faces of their children
and not their ancestors
while planning for the future.

Una O'Higgins O'Malley lives in Dublin and Oughterard. She is the second daughter of Kevin O'Higgins, Minister for Justice in the Irish Free State who was assassinated in 1927. She subsequently dedicated her public life to the cause of peace, justice and forgiveness on the island of Ireland. Her life and work is documented in her critically-acclaimed memoir *From Pardon and Protest* (Arlen House, 2001). In 2003 the same publisher brought out her first collection of poetry, *Twentieth-Century Revisited*, and in 2005 her spiritual collection, *Friends in High Places*. Una is currently editing *The Hope Anthology*.

Rita Ann Higgins

*Rita Ann Higgins read this poem at an evening in
commemoration of the life of Bríd Cummins.*

RETURN TO SENDER

One woman against the letter of the law
Irish Times December 18th 2004
(Bríd Cummins was found dead in bed
on the day she was due for eviction, Dec 6th 2004)

Our acting city manager
never stops acting
he never stops playacting.
He's a rule-book carrier
he letter-of-the-laws it
he jaw-jaws it.
He praises and praises
his full of humanity staff
his staff who gush with kindness

his staff who sing while they work
his staff who say, good morning
how may I help you?
Free from blame all the same
a councillor said, exonerated
they are all exonerated,
staff exonerated he said it again.
Another councillor said policy
policy, policy, we have to carry out council policy.
Galway city council policy.

We have to letter-of-the-law-it
we have to jaw-jaw it.

Good staff, lovely staff,
full of humanity staff
gush when we walk staff
gush when we talk staff
Staff exonerated, all exonerated.
Policy policy, letter of the law, all jaw-jaw.

Clever letter-writing member of humanity staff
writes great letter bereft of hope
sends great letter bereft of hope
to emergency housing authority 'Cope'
telling Cope to spare the hope this Christmas.

Don't re-house her
when we evict her
the clever letter writer wrote
in a clever letter sent to Cope
A clever letter bereft of hope.

She answers back
She calls back
She's a trouble maker
She's riddled with anti-social behaviour
She claims a back injury
She's always looking for repairs
and if it's not repairs it's a transfer.
She's taking legal action against us
She pisses us off
and us dribbling with humanity
we gush when we walk
we gush when we talk
we are exonerated

A councillor said so
exonerated, staff exonerated
we were carrying out council policy
Galway city council policy.

Our acting city manager
our playacting city manager
playacts on our behalf.
He has a duty to protect his staff
He has a duty to protect his back
He knows how kind we are
all year round
but especially at Christmas.

Rita Ann Higgins was born in 1955 in Galway. She published her first five collections with Salmon, *Goddess & Witch* (1990), which combines *Goddess on the Mervue Bus* (1986) and *Witch in the Bushes* (1988), *Philomena's Revenge* (1992) and *Higher Purchase* (1996). From Blackstaff in 1996 appeared *Sunny Side Plucked: New & Selected Poems*, a Poetry Book Society Recommendation, and her latest collection *An Awful Racket* (2001). Her plays include *Face Licker Come Home* (1991) and *Down All the Roundabouts* (1999). She was Galway County's Writer-in-Residence in 1987, Writer in Residence at NUI, Galway, in 1994-95, and Writer in Residence for Offaly County Council in 1998-99. In October 2000 she was Green Honors Professor at Texas Christian University. Her many awards include a Peadar O'Donnell Award in 1989 and several Arts Council bursaries. She is a member of Aosdána.

Bríd Cummins

1956-2004

Bríd was born in Clonmel on 16 February 1956, the youngest of seven children, six girls and one boy. She was educated in Clonmel, and worked in the Civil Service in Dublin and Waterford. In Brussels she was employed in the European Parliament, and, having completed a course in journalism, she worked for *Newsweek* and Reuters.

Bríd spent the last years of her life in Galway, a city she loved. She was involved in drama, art and poetry, and helped to produce and act in "Hatch 22", a play about Galway's unemployed. She edited the ground-breaking *Simon Anthology of Poetry* in 1988 which included poetry from Ireland's leading writers in aid of the Simon Community.

Bríd completed a four year course in homeopathy. Due to a disability she was unable to travel much in the last few years of her short life. She continued to write and paint and worked two days a week in the university.

Bríd died on 6 December 2004.

I tried not to look
But her icy glare sought me out.
She couldn't find anyone
More hateful than me.
She wanted to stamp on me.
Among the eggs and empty shelves
Of that just about to close
Perpetuity, she wanted
To flatten me and slide me
Through the slot of officialdom.
To be rid of me.
To shut me up,
Staple me,
File me away.
She can never forgive me.
I asked her for a receipt.

THE HAMMER MAN

If that man next door
Hammers another nail
I'll hammer him.
I'll take him on
A snowless sledge
To oblivion.
Where he can't lay his
Restless hands on
A single tool.
And the rust will
Make his joints creak,
But I won't hear them.
And bit by bit
The house he built
And rebuilt
Will stretch and sigh
On warm summer days
And whisper "thanks be to Gods"
The hammer man is gone.

Now the dancing girl
Can float in the
Limbo-land next door
And no longer
Hit the wall, or
Hit the roof, or
Hit the bottle.
And the hammer and nails
And drills and saws of
The hammerless man
Will go to rust and
Bother us no more.

AFRAID

His bed was in the corner,
By the window.
I held his hand,
Death flickered in his eyes.
He said he was afraid of
The gap in the curtains,
So the nurse pinned them
Together.
He imagined the throb of
The heart monitor
Was the sound of footsteps
In the gloom.
He was afraid
Afraid of death,
Afraid of life,
Afraid of love.
I was afraid
Of him.

A meter ticked ominously
In the tiny hallway,
A reminder of the tick-ticking
Of that monitor in the hospital ward
Where he closed his eyes and
Offered up his spirit.
The world is shot out.
A bundle of discarded newspapers
Lie on the floor, reminders of
Tragedy.
Nature's beauty dies daily
So that these informers of
Death and destruction
Can lies on floors
In sad rooms.

From a bright sunny morning
To a dim, dark night,
I have returned
To await a revelation,
Or a storm-filled hand
Through a rent in the clouds,
To whisk away the mist
From across the bay,
Which has invaded my mind
So that all I hear is
The ticking of the clocks
And meters, and monitors
Of this world without end.

Poor little lamb
Bleeds all over
My plate
I lap it up
All that blood,
Just as they lap up
My blood
As I bleed all over
This town.
They soak it up
Spew it out.
My blood.
This time I don't
Lap it up.
If I can't swim
Through it,
I'll part it
With one swift command
And
A raised hand.

LOVE'S CLOAK

I didn't know what came to me
In love's cloak.
It sat on the stairs and waited;
So anxious to meet me,
So keen to truss me up,
To influence every moment.
It waited around corners
Crouched in doorways, ready
To spring on my unsuspecting
Vulnerability.
It crawled through the long grass
On sticky summer nights, and
Sat by the river on frozen winter
Afternoons, when fools venture out.
It held me close.

On dusty city streets,
There it was again, with
A mysterious look from dark eyes,
Under a dipped hat.
It followed me through parks,
And flattered me, with offers
Of the high life.
For short periods; I succumbed,
But never comfortable
With disguise.

MOTHER

She spreads her love
Her strength
Her compassion
Throughout the family
All her living life
Loving
And guiding us
Smiles
With ready smile
Smiling.
No task too much
No load too heavy
Weighing.

Always there ready
To listen
She listens
Listening.
So understanding
So patient
So giving
Giving.
Deep thoughts
Wish words
Flow from her
Thinking.
Age seeking to alter
Her beautiful face
Beautiful.

Thickly curling
Silver hair
Graces her head
Gracefully,
Making her stature

Statuesque
Tall, grey-haired
Lady

Her warmth
So warming
Comforts
Comfortingly.
Her laugh
Cheers us all
Cheering
Cheerfully.

She's lovely
We love her
Lovingly lovely.
Loving thoughts
To a loving woman
Heart-gladdening.
Inspirational
Certainly she is
Ever inspiring.
Loved mother of mine
Forever loved
Eternally.